M000112130

How to Cultivate Collaboration in a PLC

Susan K. Sparks
Thomas W. Many

Solution Tree | Press

a division of
Solution Tree

555 North Morton Street
Bloomington, IN 47404
800.733.6786 (toll free) / 812.336.7700
FAX: 812.336.7790
email: info@solution-tree.com
solution-tree.com

Visit **go.solution-tree.com/plcbooks** to download the reproducibles in this book.

Printed in the United States of America

19 18 17 16 15   1 2 3 4 5

FSC
www.fsc.org
MIX
Paper from
responsible sources
FSC® C011935

Library of Congress Control Number: 2015938032

Solution Tree
Jeffrey C. Jones, CEO
Edmund M. Ackerman, President

Solution Tree Press
President: Douglas M. Rife
Associate Acquisitions Editor: Kari Gillesse
Editorial Director: Lesley Bolton
Managing Production Editor: Caroline Weiss
Proofreader: Elisabeth Abrams
Text and Cover Designer: Rian Anderson

With appreciation and gratitude, this work
is dedicated to Robert J. Chadwick
(May 8, 1936 – April 9, 2015)

Visit **go.solution-tree.com/PLCbooks** to
download the reproducibles in this book.

Table of Contents

About the Authors . . . . **vii**

Introduction **1**

The Obstacles 1

The Solution 1

Cultivating Collaboration in a Professional Learning Community 2

Chapter 1: Dispositions **5**

Common Issues 5

Seek Clarity and Create Commitment for Productive Behaviors
and Dispositions 6

Self-Assess and Reflect 8

Create Team Mind States 9

Focus on the Work of Student Learning 10

Chapter 2: Process **11**

Deciding Whether a Work Session Is the Right Process 12

Walking in Their Shoes: Diagnosing and Planning 13

Celebrating, Monitoring, and Honoring 19

Best Hopes and Worst Fears 20

Decision Making 22

Activities for the Different Phases of Decision Making and Teamwork . . 24

Interest-Based Strategies 33

Focusing Four 34

Keep, Drop, Create 35

Ending Meetings. 36

Protocols 36

Chapter 3: Roles and Responsibilities. 39

Facilitator. 39

Team Leader. 40

Recorder 41

Timekeeper. 41

Process Observer. 41

Summarizer. 41

Most Responsible Person 42

Team Member 42

Principal. 42

Chapter 4: Skills and Behaviors 43

Interpersonal Skills. 44

Listening and Speaking 44

Challenging Conversations. 47

Consensus and Conflict Skills 50

Data Conversation Skills 54

Chapter 5: Conclusion. 59

References. 61

About the Authors

Susan K. Sparks is an educational consultant in Denver, Colorado. Susan retired in 2008 as the executive director of the Front Range BOCES for Teacher Leadership, a partnership with the University of Colorado at Denver. Susan spent her career in St. Vrain Valley School District as a teacher and with four different boards of cooperative educational services (BOCES) as staff developer, assistant director, and executive director. She currently provides international consultation in collaborative cultures, conflict resolution, contract negotiations, and community engagement.

She provides professional development and training in facilitating professional learning communities, impacting results through interpersonal effectiveness, managing challenging conversations, and creating collaborative teams.

Susan contributed to *The Collaborative Teacher: Working Together as a Professional Learning Community* and co-authored *Leverage: Using PLCs to Promote Lasting Improvement in Schools*.

Dr. Thomas W. Many is an educational consultant in Denver, Colorado. Tom retired as the superintendent of schools in Kildeer Countryside CCSD 96 in Buffalo Grove, Illinois. Tom's career included twenty years of experience as superintendent, in addition to serving as a classroom teacher, learning center director, curriculum supervisor, principal, and assistant superintendent. During his tenure as superintendent, District 96 earned the reputation as a place where the faculty and administration worked together to become one of the premier elementary school districts in the nation.

Tom has worked with developing professional learning communities in school districts around the world. He has proven to be a valuable resource to those schools beginning their journey with special insights into developing a culture that supports the creation of high-performing collaborative teams.

In addition to nearly forty articles, Tom is the co-author of *Learning by Doing: A Handbook for Professional Learning Communities at Work, 2nd Edition* with Richard DuFour, Rebecca DuFour, and Robert Eaker; a contributing author in *The Collaborative Teacher: Working Together as a Professional Learning Community*; co-author of *Aligning School Districts as PLCs* with Mark Van Clay and Perry Soldwedel; and co-author of *Leverage: Using PLCs to Promote Lasting Improvement in Schools* with Susan Sparks-Many.

To book Susan K. Sparks or Thomas W. Many for professional development, contact pd@solution-tree.com.

Introduction

Cultivating collaboration in a professional learning community requires attention and constant care. It includes moving from isolation to collaborative teams and implementing a relentless focus on learning and results. Successful teams know that using a framework to define collaboration and high-performing teams assists them in evaluating their progress and improving their effectiveness. The five components of effective collaboration—focus, structure, process, roles and responsibilities, and relationships—were first described in "Creating Intentional Collaboration" (Sparks, 2008) and have been expanded on in our workshops and on-site coaching. We are grateful for our mentors, Richard and Rebecca DuFour, Robert Eaker, and the many educators we have learned from. We continue to learn about collaboration with each interaction and experience. We are fortunate indeed to have been associated with the best and brightest in the field of education for over thirty-five years.

The Obstacles

Teams and individuals encounter obstacles and challenges as they collaborate, including:

- Negative attitudes and unproductive behaviors
- Lack of focus and clarity, mixed messages, and an overload of initiatives
- Policies, structures, and practices focused on what is good for adults and not necessarily on what is good for student success
- Uninspired staff and team meetings
- Destructive conflict and poor communication

The Solution

The easy answer to overcoming these obstacles is to *commit to continuous improvement*! Make a promise to a thoughtful and relentless approach to team development and collaboration. Engage in and learn about practices that work. As Michael Fullan and Clif St. Germain (2006) describe in the book *Learning Places*, "What is worth fighting for is not to allow our schools to be negative by default, but to make them positive by design" (p. 19).

This book describes how teams work in detail and provides ideas and tips for cultivating collaboration. It focuses on the "how" of effective teaming. It does not include two critical components of teaming in a professional learning community (PLC): focus and structure. We recommend the many resources found within Professional Learning Communities at Work™ related to student learning and "what" the work is. One of the key questions teams must answer is, What will be the focus of our work while we're together? According to Rick DuFour, "the important question is not 'Are teachers collaborating?' but rather 'What are teachers collaborating about?'" (DuFour, DuFour, Eaker, & Many, 2010, p. 91). What has become increasingly clear is that effective teams create an unrelenting focus on the four critical questions: (1) What knowledge and skills should every student acquire? (2) How will we know when every student has acquired the essential knowledge and skills? (3) How will we respond when some students do not learn? (4) How will we extend and enrich the learning for students who are already proficient? (See "Critical Issues for Team Consideration" at **go.solution-tree.com/plcbooks**.)

Teams also create a viable and guaranteed curriculum, use formative and common assessments, and provide interventions to help all students learn. In addition to the clarity and focus, schools and teams attend to structure and organize teams by content or grade levels, provide time for teams to meet, and ensure that teams establish goals and use norms, agendas, and minutes. Leadership also provides direction and assists teams when they need help. To learn more about the work of collaborative teams in a professional learning community, see *Learning by Doing: A Handbook for Professional Learning Communities at Work* (DuFour et al., 2010) and *Leverage: Using PLCs to Promote Lasting Improvement in Schools* (Many & Sparks-Many, 2015).

Cultivating Collaboration in a Professional Learning Community

Each chapter includes a description of issues or barriers that teams encounter when collaborating and practical approaches and solutions for addressing them. In addition, resources are identified and links are included in the text to provide additional tools and strategies.

Chapter 1, "Dispositions," describes the attitudes and behaviors necessary for effective collaboration. Chapter 2, "Process," provides ideas for engaging all participants to work together in meaningful ways. Chapter 3, "Roles and Responsibilities," clarifies explicit roles and responsibilities in teams. Chapter 4, "Skills and Behaviors," elaborates on skills and behaviors that individuals and teams can improve upon in the areas of communication, consensus, managing conflict, and facilitating data conversations. Chapter 5, "Conclusion," concludes with an emphasis on collaborating for success.

Chapter 1
Dispositions

We use the term *dispositions* to describe the qualities and traits that are observable when teams are working together. They are patterns in behavior, and they have profound impacts on people as they work.

Common Issues

Why are dispositions important? Because negative or unproductive dispositions and attitudes interfere with effectiveness. These are the human behaviors that cause disruption and create lack of cohesiveness and mistrust. Not to mention that unproductive behaviors can interrupt the work and contribute to a lack of results. It is our premise that negative adult behavior should not interfere with the work of collaborative teams. What does it look like to allow behaviors to disrupt collaboration?

First, something happens—a disagreement, an action, a strong statement, a tone of voice. We may observe a positive reaction such as "I need to understand more. Let me try to understand your point of view." Or, too often, we see a negative reaction. Responses may be quick and aggressive. Comments may take on a more personal and negative tone: "I totally disagree. What a crazy idea. How did you come up with that?" In this example, unintended consequences may occur. People may shut down and not talk as openly; they may make assumptions, become upset, withdraw, and become fearful. A minor episode may escalate into a major situation, and it can temporarily stop productivity.

Collaborative work is messy, and if teammates are rolling up their sleeves and digging into the work, invariably they will say or do something that will offend or cause a ripple. It is human nature. And when a behavior turns into a routine way of acting or a predictable pattern (and the behavior is getting in the way of being productive), that is when it becomes an issue for a team.

We asked teachers to describe actions and dispositions that get in the way of collaboration. We heard:

- Gives excuses rather than takes responsibility

- Is consistently distracted

- Is habitually late or absent

- Doesn't follow through and complete tasks

- Shows bias and is judgmental

- Uses negative language

- Reacts defensively to feedback

- Doesn't listen

We could generate a more comprehensive list of undesirable qualities and add to this list. We know what we do not like. However, the key is to minimize the undesirable behavior and focus on what is desirable. The following processes will help you both prevent and intervene when such behaviors arise.

Seek Clarity and Create Commitment for Productive Behaviors and Dispositions

Schedule a conversation at the beginning of the year or during the year when your team needs a boost about working together. By being more explicit about what you desire in a team, you will have a better chance of achieving those qualities. It is much easier to have a discussion about the behaviors we struggle with and those we appreciate early in the team development process than later on when unproductive behaviors and qualities manifest inside our team work sessions. If we conduct the conversation at a safe time, it feels less targeted and personal. People are not on the defensive. It is a rational and thoughtful dialogue about what is important to each member of the team.

Purpose

The purpose of this activity is to explore what behaviors and qualities will support effective collaboration. It is designed to create a shared understanding among participants. The team does not need to reach consensus.

Steps

First, create a list of the qualities and characteristics that may get in the way of being an effective team. Each person has different triggers or irritants based on his or her own beliefs and preferences. What bothers one person may not be a struggle for another. The point is that individuals should know their own behavioral tendencies and what is conducive or destructive in their team or what teammates may react to. Every person has a perspective, and it may be different from others'. This is a safe conversation. Do not name names but rather talk about actions and behaviors.

After this conversation, it is important to move to a vision of dispositions the team desires when working together. Create a vision or a collective statement of what you do want. What beliefs, attitudes, and actions are present as we work together? This will include words from every participant, honoring each person's point of view. It is important to create a product as a result of the conversation. An example of a vision of "Dispositions We Value" is in figure 1.1.

What Are the Dispositions We Value?

Passion and commitment for teaching and learning—A core belief that all students can and will learn with appropriate time and support.

Inquisitive and growth-oriented behaviors—We thrive on challenge and are not defined by failures. We are willing to learn from others and define success by continuously learning and growing.

Inclusive—A belief in the power of the team, a true willingness to learn and explore ideas together.

Interdependent—Responsibility for and accountability to the work of the team. We depend on one another to meet the goals defined.

Transparent—Nothing is off limits in discussions, and pertinent information is shared.

Vulnerable—Acknowledgment that it isn't about having all the answers; it is about seeking help and asking for assistance.

Trustworthy—Being vulnerable with one another. "One's willingness to be vulnerable to another based on the confidence that the other is benevolent, honest, open, reliable, and competent" (Tschannen-Moran, 2004, p. 17).

Hard work ethic—Going that extra step and taking necessary time for quality work. Being perseverant and following through on tasks.

Tolerance for ambiguity—Not letting our confusion stop us from doing work. We commit to working toward clarity.

Optimistic and enthusiastic—A person who sees the possible rather than the impossible.

Positive presuppositional mindset—Assuming the best intentions when working with others.

Figure 1.1: Vision of dispositions.

Scenario

Another method of approaching the vision of working together is to forecast and think about your team in one to three years. Create a scenario (a vision of the future), and then narrow the traits and dispositions by those that are valued by all (Schwartz, 1991). Name what is happening in your team and describe how people are relating and working together. As you discuss traits, each person contributes qualities he or she wants to see and those that are most important for him or her. Again, team members do not have to agree with one another about each quality. Look for qualities that everyone does agree on, and they will become part of the final product.

Self-Assess and Reflect

Some teams prefer to use a self-assessment and discuss the results with one another before creating a vision. Phillip Newport, a literacy partner teacher in Hayward, California, interviewed with Ellen Moir about tips for the perfect PLC. He suggested that "self-reflection and group reflection happens consistently in order to bring about positive change" (Moir, 2008). It may save time and energy to begin with a list of qualities from researchers and experts in team development.

Review what behaviors and dispositions are most desirable in an effective team and determine what you want to aspire to. The following tools can help with this process.

- "Rate Yourself as a Team Player" (found at **go.solution-tree.com /plcbooks**) has a series of thirteen questions asking individuals to rate their behavior when working in a team. Participants also write three actions they can do to increase the effectiveness of their team.

- The Compass Protocol, developed by educators associated with the National School Reform Faculty and the Harmony Education Center, is similar to the Myers-Briggs Type Indicator personality inventory, helping individuals and teams clarify their preferences while communicating and working together. Participants are asked to pick a direction—north, south, east, or west—and work through a set of questions based on the descriptor associated with their direction. The activity is lively and creates more understanding among faculty and team members related to the different traits found in people. It creates more empathy and awareness for different styles. It is not meant to pigeonhole or stereotype individuals; rather, it serves to point out that each person and team has different strengths and vulnerabilities as they work. For more on Compass Protocol, visit www.nsrfharmony .org/system/files/protocols/north_south_0.pdf.

- Teams may review Daniel Goleman's (2006) work in *Emotional Intelligence*. He developed a framework of five elements including: self-awareness, self-regulation, motivation, empathy, and social skills.

- A popular self-assessment in several Colorado school districts is Emergenetics, a profile using four thinking attributes—analytical, structural, social, and conceptual thinking. These thinking attributes are combined with behavioral attributes—expressiveness, assertiveness, and flexibility. Together, they define a personality profile. Profiles are available for a fee on www.emergenetics.com.

As a team, have the conversations and discuss traits and desirable qualities. However, do not overdo it. We have heard stories of teams working for hours trying to arrive at a consensus, and it takes them away from the important work of increasing student learning.

Create Team Mind States

Once defined and practiced, teams begin to take on specific qualities and characteristics. They create their own identities and ways of working. They actually develop the dispositions as a team, and members act according to the norms of the whole. Ask administrators to describe a highly effective team in their school. They will say that the students in a particular grade level or content area are having success, and they see consistent increases in student learning. They will tell you that the team is focused and knows how to work through issues.

A body of work we have found most helpful for team reflection is the Five States of Mind, defined in the works of Arthur Costa, Robert Garmston, and Bruce Wellman and articulated in the work of Cognitive Coaching and Adaptive Schools. These states of mind are "five human capacities, or mind states, as catalysts; energy sources fueling human thinking, learning and behaviors. . . . They are the wellsprings nurturing all high-performing individuals, groups and organizations" (Costa & Garmston, 1994). The Five States of Mind are efficacy, flexibility, craftsmanship, consciousness, and interdependence (Garmston & Wellman, 2009). For more information, see "The Energy Sources Team Self-Assessment Survey" available on www. thinkingcollaborative.com.

The purpose of learning about team traits and skills is simple. We can emulate those qualities we know to be effective. We can strive and use them as a benchmark and comparison for our teams. The questions to consider are straightforward. Is our team aware of the Five States of Mind and our own areas of strength and weakness? What can we do to be more conscious of these states as we work together?

Ultimately it is acknowledgment of personal and team responsibility. What behaviors, strategies, and actions will enable us to accomplish our goals? What will we commit to?

Focus on the Work of Student Learning

In PLC at Work books and professional learning, we talk about "the right work" of teams in a PLC. The right work is focused on student learning and is the work of the team. In the All Things PLC blog (www.allthingsplc.info) posted on September 10, 2013, Anthony Muhammad stated that the most efficacious teams he has found in his ten years of research share two characteristics: (1) they discipline themselves to stay focused on the four critical questions regarding student learning, and (2) they maintain a positive atmosphere by intentionally avoiding speaking negatively about students, parents, and coworkers. If teams keep those two things in mind, they will overcome structural issues and find a way to do the right work for their students.

That intention to work in positive ways with our colleagues is often overlooked until problems arise. Teams do benefit by solidifying the values and dispositions important to them, creating norms (standards about how to treat each other), and monitoring themselves along the way. Effective teams pay attention to the adult dynamics and dispositions that enhance or tear down team effectiveness. The activities and processes provided in this chapter can be used when a team is beginning a new year, a new semester, or anytime a team needs a quick intervention. The activities and processes can be used anytime but shouldn't dominate the time set aside for collaborating. They work best when you know that something has to change to be more effective as a team—a time when you notice that the team is not doing well and you have diagnosed that it may be about issues related to beliefs, dispositions, and attitudes. One does not need a background in psychology or counseling to carry out a healthy and constructive conversation about what behaviors are getting in the way and what should be done. One needs courage, facilitation skills, and a process to manage a productive conversation.

Chapter 2
Process

We are often asked to facilitate the work of a staff or team struggling with productivity. We hear about team members being recalcitrant, not showing up or avoiding team time, acting disengaged and not taking on work, and exhibiting apathy and sometimes anger. Upon investigation, we often determine an absence of effective processes. A case study, which we will revisit throughout this chapter, illustrates this.

Ken, the principal at East Elementary School, requested help with a full staff meeting to discuss optimal practice in assessment. He wanted teachers to map their summative and formative assessments administered throughout the year by state, district, school, and course content teams and to talk about the value and purpose of each. He was responding to criticism from staff and parents about the number and reasons for the tests students were asked to take throughout the year. He had a feeling that the lack of clarity and disconnect about the scope and purposes of assessment were creating disturbances in the school and community. Ultimately, he wanted the faculty to design a "Balanced System of Assessment" for their school and in their teams (Many & Sparks-Many, 2015, pp. 62–65). He felt that the faculty should be together rather than in small teams so they could learn from one another and increase awareness. If the work session went well, it could lead to new understanding and improved practices.

When we asked questions, red flags appeared. Ken said, "The faculty has difficulty, and there are strange dynamics when they are all together. Communication feels one-way, and I talk at them more than I should. Even when I give them time and a forum to have conversations, they do not participate well." We asked some teachers about large staff conversations and work. One teacher said that comments were not always well received and she felt judged. Another said faculty meetings and professional learning days were not productive, and two stated that large-group meetings were not relevant to their everyday work. Another described that when staff met, they went round and round and did not get anywhere on a topic or with a decision. Patterns emerged that made it clear that norms were not used as a way to encourage positive adult behavior and create safety for candid conversations. There was also an absence of organization, decision making, and interactive processes to encourage productive participation.

It was clear that an increase in communication skills, a revisit of norms, and a few structural and procedural changes would assist this staff. Ken was open to suggestions and was willing to look at his own communication patterns and methods of facilitating work sessions. He agreed that the staff needed to be open and honest with one another and that ideas and concerns should be generated in public ways. He wasn't surprised with the diagnostic results and knew the culture needed to change to facilitate meaningful collaboration as a staff and in small teams. He was ready to create a new way of working with his staff and a more collaborative and open culture.

Getting this work done would require both a structure and a process. The result was a redesign of professional learning. A secondary goal was to model more effective time together so teams would use some of the same processes in their grade-level meetings. Help was enlisted from the leadership team, and we designed the work together paying special attention to the purpose and the process.

When everything flows during a meeting or work session, participants are excited and energized. Comments such as "That was a good use of time!" or "I really learned a lot!" are heard. What happens to create this energy and enthusiasm? One attribute may be that members are engaged. Another is that the process matches the goal and allows the team to accomplish their tasks. Process allows for meaningful involvement. Large staff meetings and small grade-level or content teams can have a significant and positive impact on members of the staff. Well-designed and upbeat meetings and work sessions can energize, motivate, and remind members they are part of a team. We define process as continuing actions engaged in by teachers and teams in order to achieve the desired result of increased student learning.

Deciding Whether a Work Session Is the Right Process

In *Making Meetings Work*, Ann Delehant (2007) suggests deciding whether a meeting or a work session is the best format as the first step to design: "We need to use meeting time to efficiently conduct work that advances learning goals. . . . Deciding whether a meeting is necessary is the first step in beginning to 'work smarter'" (p. 2). Use meetings when you want participation to include learning, dialogue, and decision making. Don't use meetings for dispensing information. It will sap energy. Delehant suggests using email messages, voice mail messages, video messages, informal newsletters, and weekly bulletins. In addition, effective teams use technology and electronic tools to involve others, seek responses, and generate ideas. Collaboration takes many forms, and we need to use the best process for the intended results. When you have decided to meet, ask yourself, "What do we want to accomplish, and what will create meaningful participation?"

Walking in Their Shoes: Diagnosing and Planning

One of the first jobs in designing an effective work session in small or large teams is to become clear on the goal and intended outcomes. Goals guide the work of the team. Do members of the faculty or team have the same understanding of the goals and purpose of their work? Are they clear about why they are engaged in the work? Interviewing different members will cause perspectives to surface. We hear both commonality and differences during short interviews. Ten-minute phone conversations with select members of the staff provide invaluable information and more understanding of the culture and the people involved. This information provides rich background for designing the experience. For a template on asking good questions of your team see "Diagnosis and Design for Facilitators" at **go.solution-tree.com/plcbooks**.

Walk in the participants' footsteps. If you use a series of questions to guide them through the conversation, how will they respond? If you use a protocol (a step-by-step process), will they produce the intended results? It is easy to make assumptions that the team will do this or that. Do not overthink it and assume you know exactly what the team will do. Instead, try implementing different processes and see what happens. Pay attention to both the results and the dynamics. Team members will appreciate your effort in engaging them, and they will see you working hard to meet team and individual needs.

Backward Design

Teams without direction go adrift. Purpose statements serve as a vision for the work. Start with the goal and purpose and then design backward. Most successful teams state the purpose at the beginning of the session and write it on the agenda or on a chart. When teams wander off purpose, the team leader can refer to the visual. A topic is not a purpose statement. Be careful to avoid listing topics as a purpose.

For more information, visit http://learningforward.org/docs/default-source /commoncore/tplteams.pdf (Killion, 2013) and "Diagnosis and Design for Facilitators" at **go.solution-tree.com/plcbooks**.

Linking

A useful tool and process to accompany the purpose statement is "linking." At the beginning of a meeting, describe the purpose and goal of the session, and provide context by linking it back to previous work and linking it forward to the future. This serves multiple purposes. Participants know what is expected and can focus their thinking. Linking serves as a celebration and a reminder that progress is being made. When done well, it also helps participants see the big picture and the "why" behind the work. See an example in "Team Clarity Tool" at **go.solution-tree .com/plcbooks**.

Environment

Communication is key! Ask members to sit in a circle so they can see one another and do their best work. Place one or two charts and easels next to the team, and technology should be ready if it is the preferred method for displaying data, recording, or searching for information. The rule of thumb is one easel per eight people if you plan to have them break into smaller teams to work. If you find that people only sit next to their friends, switch it up by asking them to sit in a new place or creating a process to work with different teammates. For more on logistics and environment, see Delehant (2007), pages 27–34.

Begin With Purpose and Norms

We recommend you first state the purpose and intended outcomes, review the agenda, and remind the team of the norms necessary for the conversation. Norms are the agreements we make to one another about how we will work together and treat each other. Some teams have the norms written on the agenda, on a tent card on the table, or on a chart next to them. It is OK to start by asking members to review the norms and turn to an elbow partner (the person next to them) and describe which norm will be important for them to pay attention to during the meeting. It takes one minute, and the norms have been reviewed and members are connected to their agreements. Norms, like agendas and minutes, will support a team while they are focused on student learning. For more information on creating and using norms, see *Learning by Doing* (DuFour et al., 2010), pages 136–144. For ideas on reinforcing norms and keeping them alive, see "Reinforcing Norms and Evaluating Team Effectiveness" at **go.solution-tree.com/plcbooks**.

Grounding and Check-In

Following the purpose and norms, have participants check in with a *grounding*, the term used by Robert Chadwick (2012), author and consultant in creating consensus, to describe the "round-robin" or "go around" process for checking in. Each person speaks one at a time and is not interrupted, comments or questions are not asked by other members of the team, and the person speaking takes the time needed to answer three questions: (1) What is your name, your role, and your relationship to the topic? (2) What is your expectation for the meeting? (3) How are you feeling about the topic and work for today? The questions may change depending on the needs of participants and time allowed for the session.

Some say that stating your name with people you know feels contrived. Others say that asking about feelings can derail the meeting or cause participants to stray from the task or process. However, as teams become familiar with the check-in, they count on it and do not want to skip it. It is the place for them to get connected to one another and to say something they feel is important. They also learn to do it without taking a lot of time. Try different questions for check-in and determine what works.

When designing the process, allow for sufficient time to listen to each participant, for participants to establish verbal territory, and for the facilitator to obtain needed information. The reasons for grounding and check-in are important. The process helps individuals become present and involved. It facilitates respectful listening and sends the message that each person has a voice, he or she will not be interrupted when speaking, and what he or she has to contribute is important. It also sends the message that each person is expected to contribute and be a part of the solution and task. Each person establishes verbal territory, and it will be easier to speak about other topics as the meeting continues.

There is a balance of power and energy. There is balance of logical thinking and feeling and emotional thinking. When the check-in includes both thinking and feeling questions, there is balance. There is also a sensing of energy and what is happening in the room. This helps the facilitator and the team observe and acknowledge apprehension, tension, or hidden agendas.

When each person has checked in, the facilitator summarizes the expectations and feelings, and then proceeds with the next task. If there are different expectations than the planned agenda, the facilitator acknowledges them and asks the team if the agenda needs to be changed. We do not suggest changing the agenda often, or participants may feel they can change directions on a whim or personal preference. However, if the topic or issue is getting in the way of the team accomplishing their work, a change may be needed. If a five-member team has a thirty-minute meeting time, a check-in may take three to five minutes. Teams vary the process according to the time and size of the team. Some teams comment that grounding and check-in could use too much of the meeting time. If you are worried about time, use small groups of three to four to check in and then report different or additional expectations. Model what you want from participants, and it should not be a problem. Set the tone and convey the message that each team member is important. The remainder of the work session will be more productive, and people will feel more connected. For more on how to facilitate grounding, see Chadwick (2012), pages 152–164.

Parking Lot or Issues Bin

When encountering different expectations, some facilitators will write the new topic on a chart called *Parking Lot* or *Issues Bin* and state that there is not adequate time to address it or it doesn't fit into the purpose of the meeting. The Parking Lot / Issues Bin holds items that come up and are to be addressed in future meetings. The item is "parked" but will be moved to the appropriate forum at a future time. It is important not to misuse it to park items that may be difficult or the facilitator wants to ignore. Kevin Eikenberry (2012) states that at the end of the meeting, we should go back to the Issues Bin and "address three questions: (1) Is this still an issue (or has it been resolved since it was put into the Bin)? (2) Is there an action item that can be created from this issue? If so, what is it? (3) Is this a topic that needs to be on a future meeting agenda?"

The faculty at East Elementary checked in and *grounded* at tables with these three questions. Each table had a summarizer with the job of listening for additional expectations. Additional expectations were stated out loud for everyone to hear, and the facilitator noted the new ones on a chart. They included comments such as "I would like to see us accomplish something as a faculty," "I expect to learn about different teachers' practices with assessment," "I want to know why we are doing all this testing and assessment." Ken also described his expectation that the staff speak honestly and without fear of retribution. He described his hope that the faculty would make progress and it would lead to better teaching practices and greater student learning.

The expectations chart was placed next to the purpose chart. They were not discussed or debated. They served as a guide for the rest of the meeting. At the end of the meeting, they were pointed out before participants checked out. Participants responded to the question, Did we accomplish our expectations?

Visual Dialogue

Effective teams use visuals to organize the thinking of the participants. By writing a statement or idea on a chart for all to see, the act honors the contributor. It is called *visual dialogue* or *visual recording*.

Recording visually:

- Shows collective work rather than individual work.

- Honors the contributor and clears up communication.

- Provides sense-making for the team.

- Assists in keeping a record of the work.

- Reduces repetition and stating the same thing over and over.

- Reduces tension. Focusing on something that you are creating together is productive and takes the focus from a person to a product.

- Slows the pace and the team down. Members have to wait for the words to be charted. It fosters communication.

- Is not judgmental. The contributions are what they are.
- Allows you to see the work and line up charts or pull the charts forward if you need to see past work.

Photos are taken of the charts in the order of making them. We number charts as we go. The JPEGs are turned into a PDF and put in a PowerPoint to distribute as minutes or post on a shared website. Sometimes original charts are saved to bring back into the room for ongoing work. Some teams use technology to record and project on a screen. The key is to keep the work visual and accessible.

Placement

If the charts are usually placed in one spot and you are recording a difficult or an emotional topic or issue, place the easel somewhere else to begin a new topic. A new view may change the mindset, and the simple act of repositioning can be helpful to the team. Michael Grinder (1997) talks about this in his work in *The Elusive Obvious: The Science of Non-Verbal Communication.*

Greeting and Connecting

Some teams need a little more time to establish connections to the topic and one another before diving into content or the main purpose of the meeting (especially with a difficult purpose and topic). When you have longer periods of time, you may want to use the process of *greeting.* Chadwick (2012) describes it as one of the oldest forms of communication, to greet and be greeted. We noticed that some teams need to disrupt old habits. Some sit in the same spot, time after time, and talk only with those they know. Others come in with tasks like grading to complete during a meeting. Interactive processes will help you address some of these issues, and they will also expand the community.

After a grounding and check-in, we ask individuals to stand and meet with another person from a different table. Once they introduce themselves, we ask them to answer one question or respond to a statement one person at a time. Again, we reiterate listening with intention, and not interrupting by asking questions or turning the conversation to our own desires. Once the first person is done, the partner will answer the same question from his or her point of view. The questions can be personal or professional, content driven with a focus on meeting purpose, or something more challenging. Time each round to one to two minutes per person, and then ask them to change partners and begin again with a new partner and a new question or statement. After three rounds, participants go back to their seats. We finish by asking them to answer two questions at their tables: What did you learn that will help you in your work, and how did you feel about it? It is also important to add insights about listening and learning at this time.

We used the "stand and connect" process with three questions for East Elementary staff.

1. Describe a time (anytime during your life) when you took a test or an assessment and you felt like it was authentic and accurately depicted what you knew and could do. Describe what it was and how you felt about it as a learner.

2. Describe the different methods you use to check for understanding and learning in your classroom.

3. Think about the learning and the progress of students in your classroom. What are you most excited about?

After each question, participants changed partners and had to find people from tables other than their own. Upon completion, individuals expressed the following statements at their table teams.

- "I learned that we have more in common than I thought."

- "I learned that if we spend time talking to each other, we will be able to improve our practices."

- "I learned that I make assumptions about what other people may think and I need to quit doing that."

- "I learned a new method for checking for learning, and I am trying it tomorrow."

- "I learned that I rarely make time to talk to someone outside my grade level, and I need to broaden my circle."

- "I learned that I am shy and talking one on one is a difficult activity for me."

- "I learned that we have passion as a staff around learning, and it will help us address the issues we have."

We do not record insights. We just report out. Reporting out begins to feel normal and encourages more participation. We model acceptance and do not judge or react to comments. Sometimes, members share something negative or hard for them. We want them to do this to increase vulnerability and transparency in the team. After the connecting activity, we challenge participants to continue to seek out new people and other points of view, to sit in different places in meetings and learn from each other. Taking fifteen to twenty minutes for grounding and greeting establishes a tone and new ways of relating to one another. Chadwick (2012) reminds us that it is important to take time to do what needs to be done. By establishing the norm of listening through grounding and greeting and following it with processes to involve team members, the rest of the work becomes more efficient and effective. Team members know each other on more personal levels and begin to open up and build trust.

In addition to improving participation, we build in celebration and a focus on what is working. *Learning partner* is a term coined from the work of Robert Garmston and Bruce Wellman (2009) in *The Adaptive School*. The process requires participants to move out of their comfort zone and connect with people from across the room. For more ideas on creating random partners, see the work of Gayle H. Gregory and Lin Kuzmich (2007) in *Teacher Teams That Get Results*, pages 45–48. For more about greeting, see Chadwick (2012), pages 175–186 and 193–198.

Be Strategic

In a five-member team, you can vary the processes of grounding and connecting and reduce time and the number of questions. For instance, you may not use the connecting activity each meeting, or you may use one question. Integrate connecting activities when you sense a need to build listening skills or to work on relationships and culture. Make sure connecting is purposeful and explain the "why" behind using it.

Celebrating, Monitoring, and Honoring

As DuFour et al. (2010) tell us, "Recognition must be specifically linked to the purpose, vision, collective commitments, and goals of the organization if it is to play a role in shaping culture" (p. 39). Celebrating small and big wins is essential in building a culture of excellence. Frequent recognition of the efforts and achievements of both adults and students is a powerful motivating force. Tom Peters and other management gurus describe celebrating what you want to see more of. Celebrations reinforce work and values, leading to continued effort. It keeps the community energized and resourceful. Timothy Kanold (2011) writes in *The Five Disciplines of PLC Leaders* about the synchronous nature of celebration and accountability.

> Well-led celebrations, moments that are used to extol or praise others, also serve the dual purpose of accountability. Leaders well trained in the discipline of accountability and celebration embrace celebrating student achievement results *and* adult actions that are consistent with and advance the vision and values of the district, school, or school program. (p. 38)

Monitoring the results and work takes a deliberate approach and a commitment to stay present and notice what is happening in your team and in your school. Monitoring with an eye on results and accountability is everyone's responsibility and can be accomplished by building in time to ask poignant questions of your team such as "What gains have we seen in student learning in . . .?" and "What specific strategies are contributing to success?" Teams also become clear on what is tight and loose in their team when it comes to clarity and monitoring what they want to see more of. Most successful teams do not leave monitoring and celebration to chance.

Four Keys for Incorporating Celebration Into the Culture of Your School or District

1. Explicitly state the purpose of celebration.
2. Make celebration everyone's responsibility.
3. Establish a clear link between the recognition and the behavior or commitment you are attempting to encourage and reinforce.
4. Create opportunities for many winners. (DuFour et al., 2010, pp. 38–39)

Honoring is a term from Chadwick (2012) and is intended to refer to honoring actions and contributions by team members. It is simple. The facilitator or designated team member states he or she would like to honor a fellow teammate. The person states who it is and describes his or her contributions. In a larger gathering, we ask the person being honored to stand in the middle of the room or circle so all can see him or her during the recognition. The rest of the team adds more content or applauds, and the meeting moves on. Honoring creates community and a team. It helps members know that their actions are important and their hard work is appreciated. An impromptu speech is the best. Use specific, heartfelt, and sincere comments. For more ideas on celebrating, see *Learning by Doing* (DuFour et al., 2010), pages 37–41, and *Creating a Culture for Learning* (Rutherford et al., 2011), pages 98–105.

Best Hopes and Worst Fears

Another process teams may use to express both their fears and hopes about an issue, a change, or an initiative is a process adapted from Chadwick (2012). This process allows individuals to publicly express what may never be said publicly but is under the surface and creates tension. *Best hopes and worst fears* is a process used to create a vision for the future (hopes) and a list of cautions or concerns (fears). The fears are reminders of past experiences and what may get in the way of progress and work. People tend to think about worst fears and may not be as productive because they are consumed by thinking about them. We recognize fears, but we do not focus on them.

After the East Elementary team explored assessment practices and talked about the different assessments administered at different levels from national tests to classroom formative checks for understanding and learning, the facilitator asked each person to pick out a 3 × 5 card on their table. On one side, they wrote down the answer to the following question: What is your worst fear about creating a balanced system of assessment in our school and in your team? After finishing, they were asked to write on the reverse side of the card and respond to: What is your best hope for creating a balanced system of assessment in our school and in your team? The facilitator then asked each person to read exactly what was on his or her card for *worst fears* only to the table group followed by the next person and the next. There was no discussion or agreement about what was written. (Note: When using this in conflict or when you feel the team needs it, a recorder for each table team writes the exact words on a chart. This slows the team down with each response honored by writing it on the chart.) Comments for East Elementary included:

- "My worst fear is that I will have to redo everything I have been doing for years."
- "I will find out that my kids are doing worse than I thought."
- "That we will try this for a week or two and then never follow through."

We talked about how worst fears are often based on our past experiences and drive our energy and actions in the present. Sometimes fears become our reality by acting in a self-fulfilling prophecy. Next, members were asked to read their *best hopes* in the same manner they read their fears. There was a definite energy shift in the room with higher, louder, and more enthusiastic voices. Statements included:

- "My best hope is that we will have more clarity, and I will not feel so overwhelmed because at least I will know why we are doing what we are doing."
- "Our school and team will be able to help more students, and more students will be successful."
- "I will do a better job as a professional with my kids."

We talked about how best hopes become our collective vision. Sometimes they do not feel as real to us as fears because we may not have had experiences with them. They can feel like a dream or a faraway goal. However, the hopes will drive the team's work and actions. We will focus on fostering strategies and actions to support the hopes.

Over the years, we have heard high-performing teams state, "Are we acting on our hopes or our fears?" They have been able to change the negative conversation and turn it around by asking that one question. It is a powerful process and shifts the focus and energy of a team. The next question asked after this process is, What beliefs, actions, and behaviors will foster best hopes? People also ask, "What do you do with the fears?" We put both hopes and fears into a collective statement. Teams should review the collective statement midway through the project and ask themselves, "Are we operating based on fear or hope? Do our actions match our hopes?" A discussion occurs about how to continue to move in a positive direction. To facilitate best hopes, see Chadwick (2012), pages 252–260, and for more on collective statements, see Chadwick (2012), pages 354–369 and "Developing Collective Statements" at **go.solution-tree.com/plcbooks**.

Decision Making

All teams must determine how they make decisions and what it looks like when they agree on something. As described in our case study, the faculty did not use norms and had not defined their decision-making process. It created ripples and disillusioned faculty members. Think about your team. Do you use a fair and valid process to make decisions? Is it the loudest voice or the last voice on a topic that determines the direction? We suggest teaching all staff about types of decisions and then deciding as a faculty (and then as a team) the type, the process you will use, the indicators of when you have or do not have agreement, and how you will communicate the decision.

Types of Decisions

An *autocratic decision* describes when one person makes a decision and does not consult or gather input first. Principals and teachers make autocratic decisions daily. Examples include schedule changes or calling a parent about a student. Autocratic decisions are quick and save time and energy.

The next type of decision includes gathering input and information. This is a *consultative method* and is used frequently when time is of the essence. The person gathering input will ultimately make the decision. An example may be building a master schedule or determining the composition of collaborative teams. With consultative decision making, it is important to explicitly state that you seek input but you will make the decision. We have heard staff make comments like, "Why did she ask me if she was going to do what she wanted anyway?" Having conversations with staff about how we make decisions and that ideas will be considered but the final decision may not be the one suggested is important. More trust builds when the person seeking input is clear about this and honors the words and work of those providing input when explaining the final decision.

Some decisions are made with a *majority* supporting the idea. This is the democratic way, and yet it may not yield support and ownership of the solution. An example is asking the staff to vote on when they want to schedule a conference day. The top vote getter will be the agreement. Staff understand the majority way of making decisions and may be able to quickly move on once a vote has occurred, but some may feel that a certain majority is running the school.

Modified consensus is the preferred form of decision making in collaborative teams and PLCs. It takes more time, and yet it yields benefits to an action orientation of PLC.

Consensus

Consensus, as defined in *Learning by Doing* (DuFour et al., 2010),

> establishes two simple standards that must be met in order to move forward when a decision is made. A group has arrived at consensus when:
>
> 1. All points of view have not merely been heard, but actively solicited.
> 2. The will of the group is evident even to those who most oppose it. (p. 228)

When we work with a staff or team, we also make sure everyone has had an opportunity to voice his or her opinion, a fair and valid process was used to analyze and determine the recommendation, and it is clear that the proposal is supported by the will of the group.

A norm attached to consensus is that members will support the decision publicly and will refrain from talking about it in a negative manner with others. Each member will commit to implementation and gather information about its effectiveness in a fair and balanced manner.

Temperature Checks and Polls Along the Way

Sometimes teams are not ready to make a final decision or recommendation, yet they want to know how others feel about an idea. If this is the case, ask for a temperature check or poll the team. Talk about the idea thoroughly and call for a temp reading. Ask, "Who supports this idea as a direction?" Ask the individuals who do not support it to talk about their concerns and ideas for addressing them. Look for patterns, areas of agreement, differences, and more options. At this stage, it is good to ask about mutual gain (Rutherford et al., 2011).

Indicators of Agreement

Effective teams use a method for showing their support for or against an idea. The "fist to five" strategy can give you information. Members rate their support: 5—I fully support this and will be a spokesperson and champion for it; 4—I strongly agree with this proposal; 3—The proposal is OK with me, and I am willing to go along; 2—I have reservations and am not ready to support it; 1—I am opposed to this proposal; fist—If I had the authority, I would veto this proposal. For more on fist to five, see *Learning by Doing* (DuFour et al., 2010), pages 227–229.

We use the thumbs-up method for checking for agreement. A thumb up means "I support this and am good with it," a thumb sideways means "I support it, but I do have some concerns," and a thumb down means "I am not ready to support it or do not agree with the direction." If anyone shows a thumb sideways or down, he or she will speak about his or her concerns. The individual or team tries to address some of the concerns by brainstorming more ideas, providing additional information about the strengths of the recommendation, asking more questions, or continuing to shape the recommendation. It is useful to split the recommendation into parts members can agree to and parts they cannot.

Remember what the definition for consensus is. When it is time for the team to move on, the person with concerns will need to let go if the will of the team is clear. Letting go means to go with the will of the team and try the proposal for the agreed-upon time. Often we will hear a statement such as "It wasn't my preferred choice, but I see that the team supports it and I will try it."

At East Elementary, Ken began the day stating the purpose and that the final product needed consensus support by the staff. He added a decision-making norm and defined consensus as having 75 percent of the staff supporting the idea. The staff agreed that the process would be respectful, with each person having the opportunity for input. The staff also discussed supporting the decision once it was made. The members commented on the value of using this method and that it would help the faculty be more efficient and effective with their time. Ken asked the staff to use consensus as defined and the process as described. It would be evaluated over time. When it was time to decide, the staff used the method of thumbs-up and found themselves in consensus with the next steps and planned actions for creating the framework. It provided a direction and a sense of accomplishment.

Activities for the Different Phases of Decision Making and Teamwork

"People support that which they create." This adage comes to us from the school team approach implemented in the 1980s for working together in schools on drug and alcohol prevention. It implies that people must be part of the conversation, the learning, and the creation to support direction and decisions. People seek a voice in issues related to what affects them. We promote processes that honor those needs. Faculty and teams must make decisions on a continual basis. Some are autocratic, some consultative, and some made with consensus. When you seek support and ownership for a decision, use the consensus approach and a step-by-step process for exploring, analyzing, and creating the solution. Even the most reluctant and disagreeable staff members become team members working on a common goal when they believe they are involved in a fair and meaningful process that is relevant to them. There are different methods used to make decisions, and teams may use something as simple as listing ideas and then talking about benefits for and concerns against each. Some teams find pluses and minuses are not as helpful and may need a process that will allow for more dialogue and learning before making a decision. Most decision-making processes will lead a team through the following stages.

1. Learning and gathering information including conducting research and building shared knowledge

2. Defining the problem, clarifying, and understanding other points of view (expanding our thinking)

3. Generating ideas and possibilities

4. Categorizing and narrowing options

5. Prioritizing and deciding

6. Evaluating and discussing observable results

7. Action planning

Following are processes and ideas for teams to use as they experience each phase.

Learning and Gathering Information Including Conducting Research and Building Shared Knowledge

Following are activities for the first phase of decision making. Use these when teams need to learn together, or explore a variety of approaches and for sharing background information.

Jigsaw (Aronson & Patnoe, 2011)

1. Divide an article into parts, and create a poster or visual with the directions.

2. Create learning teams of three to four, and number off with each taking a number that corresponds to part of the text.

3. Each person reads his or her section, highlights, and looks for big ideas (he or she will be teaching the learning team the content).

4. All number ones meet in one corner of the room with their expert group and talk about the big ideas. All number twos meet in a different area, all number threes in a different area, and so on.

5. After talking, they bring back their knowledge and teach their learning team.

6. After teaching, teams discuss the implications for their situation.

Say Something in Trios (adapted from Lipton & Wellman, 2004)

1. Create a small team (three participants), and number off.

2. Everyone takes a few minutes and reads and highlights three to four key concepts from a text or a list.

3. Team member 1 describes one of the key concepts he or she selected and says something about it.

4. Team member 2 follows by saying something about the key idea from team member 1's idea. Team member 3 follows saying something about team member 1's idea too.

5. Repeat the process with team member 2 starting with a new concept.

6. Repeat with team member 3.

Last Word (Easton, 2009)

1. Each person in a group of four reads and selects a significant passage.

2. The first participant reads the passage out loud. He or she says nothing more and does not describe why he or she picked it.

3. The other three participants have one minute each to respond to the passage.

4. The first participant then has three minutes to state why he or she chose that passage and respond to the other participant comments.

5. The same pattern is followed with a second participant with a new passage.

Text Rendering (Larner, 2007)

1. Ask participants to read an excerpt or section of an article or book and find a passage that is significant.

2. In round one, each person shares a significant sentence, and it is recorded.

3. In round two, each person shares a significant phrase, and it is recorded.

4. In round three, each person shares a significant word, and it is recorded.

5. The participants discuss new insights about the text.

4As: Agreement, Assumption, Argue, and Aspire To

1. Each participant reads and marks the following passages, sentences, or concepts.

    - + Something I agree with

    - – Something I would argue with

- ◆   * Assumptions the author holds true

- ◆   ! Something I aspire to

2. Using a round-robin, each person states one of his or her Agrees. Continue until you finish the Agrees, then go to Argues, and each person again states one of his or her Argues until you have shared each. Continue the same process with Assumptions and Aspires To. Dialogue follows after listening to each share without interruption from others.

Here's What, So What, Now What (Thompson-Grove, 2004)

This starts with gathering information and moves to different phases of decision making.

1. Look at data and answer, "Here's what . . ." stating what you found, using fact statements.

2. Now move to "So what," and discuss implications.

3. Move to "Now what," and determine what to do about it and create a plan of action.

Action Research (Sagor, 2000, p. 3)

Educational action research can be engaged in by a single teacher, by a group of colleagues who share an interest in a common problem, or by the entire faculty of a school. Whatever the scenario, action research always involves the same seven-step process. These seven steps, which become an endless cycle for the inquiring teacher, are the following:

1. Selecting a focus
2. Clarifying theories
3. Identifying research question
4. Collecting data
5. Analyzing data
6. Reporting results
7. Taking informed action

Defining the Problem, Clarifying, and Understanding Other Points of View (Expanding Our Thinking)

Following are activities for the second phase of decision making. This phase is about getting clear and understanding different perspectives.

Panels (Chadwick, 2012)

1. Select four to five people with diverse points of view. They will be called the panel and may sit in their same seats within a circle.

2. Ask each panel member to speak for three to five minutes. Ask them to describe their own perspective on the following questions: How do you view the situation (what is currently happening), and how do you feel about it?

3. Divide the audience into small groups, and distribute panel members to each small group. They become facilitators. Each group answers the prompt, "What I heard the panel members(s) say, how I feel about it, and what I learned."

4. Others who have not expressed how they see the situation may add their perspective in small groups.

Critical Inquiry Process
The group answers the following questions.

1. What are we doing now?

2. How did we come to be this way?

3. Whose interests are being served by the way things are?

4. What information do we have or need that bears upon the issue?

5. What are we going to do about all of this?

Go Around, or Round-Robin (Kaner, Lind, Fisk, & Berger, 2007)

1. Start with one person and ask him or her to respond to a question or prompt.

2. Move to the next person, and so on. Participants may pass.

3. Next time, you may reverse the order to enhance the balance.

Listeners and Summarizers (Chadwick, 2012)
Before beginning a dialogue or conversation, ask for two to three listeners. Their job is to listen and summarize what they hear from fellow colleagues. They do not add their opinion or perspective; they paraphrase and use the words of those speaking.

Walking in a Stakeholder's Footsteps (adapted from Kaner et al., 2007)

1. Mix participants up, and ask them to answer a thought-provoking question from the viewpoint of a student, teacher, parent, senior citizen, community member, administrator, and so on. They may write ideas on charts after organizing their thinking in role-alike groups.

2. Follow up with a question such as, What did we hear? or What did we learn that may impact our work?

Generating Ideas and Possibilities

The purpose of this phase is to formulate possibilities, ideas, and opportunities. "Brainstorming honors the expertise that exists within the person or group, recognizes that most problems have more than one possible solution, and prevents us from prematurely selecting the first solution that comes to mind" (Sparks, 2005, p. 17).

Freewheeling Brainstorming (Delehant, 2007, p. 135)

In this form of brainstorming, the group makes use of free associating and lists all ideas that are offered. Participants do not evaluate or discuss the ideas. Repetition is OK; the goal is quantity.

Carousel Brainstorming (Delehant, 2007)

1. Divide participants into equal-numbered groups.

2. Put charts on the wall or at the table of each group.

3. Write a topic, question, or extended sentence at the top of each chart.

4. Each group brainstorms and writes answers to the prompt.

5. At a signal, they move (clockwise) to the next chart.

6. At the end, have a gallery walk, during which participants circulate and read everyone's responses.

Infinity Brainstorming (adapted from Delehant, 2007)

1. Give a stack of sticky notes to each participant.

2. Ask a question, and provide quiet time for each person to write as many ideas or responses to the question (one idea per sticky note) he or she can think of.

3. Once complete, ask table teams to organize the sticky notes in categories on a chart and label the categories.

4. Have each team share with the large group, and look for patterns, similarities, and differences.

Mail Call

1. Provide envelopes to teams with four blank index cards inside.

2. Determine the "mail routes," how each envelope will be passed to another team. They should be passed at least three or four times to different teams.

3. Each team writes a problem of practice on the outside of the envelope.

4. At the signal, they pass the envelope to another team. Every table has a new envelope and reads the problem of practice, takes out one index card, and as a team, brainstorms solutions or ideas to solve the problem.

5. After two minutes, the cards are put back into the envelope and passed to the next table.

6. Once the cards inside are complete with different ideas from different tables, the original team receives their envelope and reads all the different suggestions and ideas.

Categorizing and Narrowing Options

Following are activities for the fourth phase of decision making.

Circles and Colors

Use this activity to categorize brainstormed ideas or information from different teams.

1. Line up posters containing brainstormed ideas in the front of the room and ask, "What ideas are the same or similar?" Those who contributed the ideas must agree it is OK to put them together.

2. Use a different-colored marker per idea to circle or check so you can see the categories emerging. You may wish to use a new chart to organize the ideas or categories.

Criteria Matrix (Garmston & Wellman, 2009)

This activity is used to evaluate possible solutions to a problem, based on pre-determined criteria.

1. Write the criteria on the left side of a chart. Agree on the criteria.

2. Across the top, write the solutions the group is considering.

3. Check off whether each solution meets the criteria identified. A variation is to number 1–5 to evaluate the degree to which the criterion meets each possible solution.

80/20 Principle (Sparks, 2005)

1. Review the list of options.

2. Apply the 80/20 principle (80 percent of the benefits will be found among 20 percent of the items on the list).

3. Determine which items are likely to produce the maximum benefit.

Nominal Group Technique (Rutherford et al., 2011)

1. Identify the problem or issue.

2. Individuals write ideas or solutions to the problem on note cards.

3. Each person reports out, one idea at a time, and records the idea on a flip chart. Ideas can be clarified as they are shared or after all are recorded.

4. Each person writes four to five ideas he or she feels are best from the list on a note card.

5. Record the number of votes next to each on the list.

6. The items with the most votes are discussed in more detail.

Balanced Sheets (Delehant, 2007)

1. Create a T-chart with a solution on the top of a chart, pluses (pros) in the left column, and minuses (cons) in the right column.

2. The team analyzes the pros and cons of implementation.

Devil's Advocate (Delehant, 2007)

1. After brainstorming solutions, ask members to play devil's advocate and offer dissenting opinions about a solution, making sure to cover all angles and aspects.

2. Before you begin, clarify norms and make sure that team members understand that this is an activity to prevent premature decisions or groupthink.

Prioritizing and Deciding

Following are activities for the fifth phase of decision making and can be difficult for teams. By using a process, the team does not get stuck and they begin to see which options are rising to the top of the list. To conclude this stage, the team must use the thumbs up or fist to five to show which option will become the proposal.

Force Field Analysis (Delehant, 2007)

1. State the current situation and a proposed change.

2. Participants identify forces that are enhancing or supporting that change (driving forces) on the left side of a chart.

3. Participants list forces that are blocking the desired change or achievement of the goal on the right side.

4. Participants may further determine the weight of each, totaling 100 percent on each side.

5. Participants examine how to minimize powerful restraining forces and promote driving forces.

Weighted Voting (adapted from Delehant, 2007)

1. Give participants an opportunity to select their favorite or high-priority items from a list posted on a chart.

2. Provide five dots (stickers) to each person. He or she can place the dots anywhere they choose (all on one item or spread out among items). A variation is to provide $1.00 to each participant, and he or she can spend all of it on one idea or divide it.

3. Once everyone has voted, add up the numbers on each item, and see what rises to the top.

4. For privacy and anonymity, call for a break, and ask people to vote during the break, or you can turn the chart stands around (not facing the group) so the voting is less public.

Paired Comparisons or Forced Choice (Delehant, 2007)

1. After reviewing and clarifying options, analyze each option against another.

2. After discussing the merits of each, every person must choose one of the two.

3. Follow the process for each option. Several will drop off the list.

4. Options surviving elimination remain possible options for the team to consider.

Commitment Continuum (Delehant, 2007)

1. Chart the proposal and seek clarification. Ensure shared understanding on the option.

2. Provide dots and ask each person to place his or her dot on "yes" or "no" or on a scale of 1–10 (1 is strong disagreement, "I think this is a mistake," and 10 is strong agreement, "I think this is the best option").

3. Provide a different-colored dot. Ask each person to rate his or her level of contribution and support on the same scale 1–10 (1 is minimal support, and 10 is maximum support).

Evaluating and Discussing Observable Results

Following is an activity for defining results.

Defining Results

Define results, and create SMART goals. For more information on writing short-term and long-term SMART goals, see *The Handbook for SMART School Teams: Revitalizing Best Practices for Collaboration* (Conzemius & O'Neill, 2014). Also see www.greenville.k12.oh.us/Downloads/SMART-Goals-Web-2013.pdf for more information on setting SMART goals.

Action Planning

Following are activities for the final stage of decision making.

Theory of Action

Theory of action is a proposed set of assumptions about how the actions will accomplish the purposes. For more on the theory of action, see *Leading for Results* (Sparks, 2005), pages 37–39.

Action Planning (Delehant, 2007)

1. Analyze the problem and issues.

2. Define goals.

3. Identify objectives.

4. Identify obstacles.

5. Develop strategies.

6. List action steps and timelines.

7. Implement the action plan.

8. Assess the solution.

A helpful resource is *The Adaptive School* (Garmston & Wellman, 2009). There are over 150 different methods for activating and engaging groups, exploring and discovering, and organizing and integrating. Another source with a more condensed list is "Interactive Tools and Strategies" at **go.solution-tree.com/plcbooks**.

Interest-Based Strategies

Another popular process for approaching an issue or major decision is to use the interest-based strategies (IBS) method used by the North American Association of Educational Negotiators and the National Education Association and modeled after the integrative negotiation model and the interest-based relational approach.

It has been used throughout the United States in districts as a win-win model for negotiations and for exploring bigger issues associated with structures to support education and PLC implementation. IBS involves six stages.

1. Telling the story and describing the situation in detail

2. Listing all the interests of those involved (interests are why this is important to the person or why it needs to be resolved)

3. Brainstorming options

4. Creating criteria for measuring the options

5. Creating a proposal of the best option or options that meet the criteria and as many interests as possible

6. Creating a plan to implement and evaluate the recommendation

IBS works well for new initiatives, changes, or problems. Moving through the six distinct steps leads to new understanding and creativity. For more information, see "Interest-Based Description" at **go.solution-tree.com/plcbooks**.

Focusing Four

Another step-by-step decision-making process is called *focusing four* and was developed by Robert Garmston and Bruce Wellman (2009). The process involves four steps.

1. **Brainstorming:** Recording all ideas on charts.

2. **Clarifying:** Asking clarifying questions related to the ideas; not making statements but asking the author to elaborate and clarify.

3. **Advocating:** Using brief and positive statements to describe support for items team members want to consider.

4. **Canvassing:** Asking each team member to identify which items are most important. Usually members are asked to select one-third plus one of the items that are listed. For example, if there are fifteen ideas, each person can select six items. Checks can be placed next to each item, and the team will begin to see what items are most important or generate the most interest. This process helps teams narrow choices and is a positive approach to seeing what is most important to the team.

Keep, Drop, Create

An approach to working on standards and curriculum together is the Keep, Drop, Create approach (DuFour et al., 2010). Teachers meet once a quarter to determine essential learning for their course and grade level and to analyze the intended versus the implemented curriculum.

> Each member of the team brings his or her lesson plan books and a copy of the essential curriculum. Three pieces of butcher paper are posted on the wall of the meeting room and labeled with one of the three categories: Keep, Drop, or Create. Each member of the team is then given sticky notes in three colors—yellow for Keep, pink for Drop, and green for Create—and is asked to reflect honestly on his or her teaching.
>
> Teams begin their analysis using their lesson plan books as the record of what was actually taught (the implemented curriculum) and copies of state or district curriculum guides to review the intended curriculum. Topics identified in the essential curriculum documents and included in each teacher's lesson plan book are recorded on the Keep page. Topics identified as essential but not addressed in the teacher's lesson plan book (either because the topics have not yet been taught or because they have been omitted) are listed on the Create page. Finally, topics included in a teacher's lesson plan book but not reflected in the essential curriculum documents are put on the Drop page.
>
> The process not only assists in discovering curriculum gaps and topics that must be addressed in upcoming units, it also helps teams create a "stop doing" list of topics that are not essential. As teachers engage in this activity over time, they become clear, more consistent, and more confident in their response to the question, "What must our students know and be able to do as a result of this unit we are about to teach?" (DuFour et al., 2010, pp. 65–66)

See directions and a template for this activity at www.allthingsplc.info/files/uploads/mathchingclassroom.pdf.

Teachers appreciate the process because it creates transparency and assists in what could be a difficult conversation. Having the information posted keeps it organized, and teachers have commented that it is more efficient each time they use it. Once the information is posted, the conversation follows about what to do. Decisions must be made. Teams may use a variation of focusing four describing what they think is most important to "keep" by clarifying, advocating, and canvassing. They would repeat the process with "drop" and "create." See "Aligning the Curriculum and Common Assessments" at **go.solution-tree.com/plcbooks**.

Ending Meetings

A good ending of a meeting or work session summarizes the accomplishments and challenges of the team, describes next steps and work to be done, and gathers honest feedback. Honest feedback models transparency and provides information for continuous improvement. Ending meetings can be a time for community, relationship building, and celebration. Participants will walk out feeling connected. Recommended quick processes are:

- Plus/Delta T-Chart—Go back to the purpose of the meeting, and record input on what worked on the left side of the chart and ask what needs to be improved on the right side of the chart.

- Conduct a quick go around / round-robin with each person checking out with one short statement or phrase. He or she selects *one* of the following statements to respond to: What is encouraging to you about the work of the team? What do you believe the team needs to continue to work on? What have you learned or relearned? What are you excited about? What are you concerned about? See "Ending the Meeting and Evaluating Effectiveness" at **go.solution-tree.com/plcbooks**.

When using a process that matches the purpose, it will likely lead to desired results. Teams should try a variety of processes. They will find some more effective than others. The key is results orientation through interaction and participation. Ask, "How will members of the team be involved and engaged?"

Protocols

It is clear that time with peers focused on the right work is not an option and is a necessity, and finding that time for collaboration can be challenging. However, ensuring that the time is used effectively can be just as daunting. Protocols are tools used to promote more efficiency and effectiveness during collaborative time. A protocol consists of a structured format that includes a time frame and specific guidelines for communication among team members. Descriptions of protocols typically identify the purpose, steps in the process, time required, expected outcomes, and roles of team members. Protocols are designed to promote the examination of student work and to reflect on a teacher's pedagogy. Some protocols facilitate the analysis of data while others focus on the examination of a lesson. There are protocols that generate suggestions for setting goals with students; others analyze the relationship between lessons, standards, and rubrics. Many protocols enable teachers to collect data, make comparisons, and track student progress. Still others delve deeply into the quality of a teacher's pedagogy and identify strategies for improving an assignment, project, or assessment.

Using protocols will assist in building a sense of community among and between teachers. Teams participate in professional, learner-focused conversations, and the structure serves as a co-facilitator helping teams stay focused on the right work. More trust becomes a by-product of using protocols.

National Turning Points: Center for Collaborative Education argues that looking collaboratively at student work and participating in collective problem solving through the use of protocols move teachers away from the isolating concept of "my students" and toward the community concept of "our students." Teams should expect some dubious responses as teams begin to use protocols. "It's scary work, though, and respectful protocols can help" (Weaver-Dunne, n.d.). When teachers are asked to share their student scores and results, they may feel intimidated and reluctant. Results may be threatening, and that is exactly why protocols can be useful. It gives teachers a step-by-step process, a product to focus on, and direction. Like other interactive processes, you may see pushback because it interrupts the normal way of talking and working. The process may feel stiff and take longer. Teams need to persevere and try different protocols in different settings and evaluate the benefits.

Like most changes, as teachers gain experience with using protocols, their confidence and comfort levels increase, as do the realized benefits. The use of protocols will make teacher teams more productive. Further, teachers must recognize that a protocol is a means to an end—not an end in itself. Stevi Quate (personal communication, 2005) cautions, "The point is not to do the protocol well, but to have an in-depth, insightful conversation about teaching and learning." For more information on protocols, visit the Free Resources from the National School Reform Faculty at the Harmony Education Center (www.nsrfharmony.org).

As more interactive tools and processes were used in the East Elementary work session, teachers spoke up, were candid, and were able to describe some of their frustrations and hopes. Some of the behaviors noted in the diagnosis about not participating and feeling like meetings were a waste of time were not reflected in the observations or in the evaluations. Designing with an end in mind and creating authentic dialogue and participation made a difference. The work session was successful, and participants commented that goals were met, the team had ideas for a draft of an assessment framework for their school, and they had an opportunity to learn about something relevant and important to them. There were still some concerns about follow-through and whether collaboration would continue after the day.

This was important feedback to leadership. The good news was that even the concerns expressed by individuals in the check-out were public and sincere. They were expressed and not suppressed. There was a respectful tone with all participants, and the day provided a launch for continued conversation and productive collaboration.

Chapter 3
Roles and Responsibilities

The most effective teams have identified roles and responsibilities to avoid confusion and resentment. If team roles and responsibilities are not defined when teams are working, processes and meetings can fall flat. Reoccurring problems in teams include the confusion of who does what and individuals feeling they have to do it all themselves, and the work not being shared and fairly distributed, creating an imbalance in the workload. Such an atmosphere may create disorganization and poor productivity, leading to resentment and frustration. Identifying team roles and responsibilities may clear up the ambiguity and create more balanced and shared ownership of the work. The key to success is to define and describe each role, evaluate the effectiveness periodically, and share roles over time.

Facilitator

According to Joellen Killion (2013),

> Facilitators . . . create the conditions and supportive environments in which people are comfortable collaborating. They manage time, people, and resources, and support interpersonal relationships to help individuals and the team achieve their goals.
>
> **A facilitator helps the team** free itself from internal obstacles or difficulties so members may more efficiently and effectively accomplish their goals.
>
> **A facilitator guides the team's work** without directing it, helps the team discover ways to address challenges and maintains safety and trust among members.

A facilitator brings structures and processes to help the team accomplish its goals.

A facilitator appreciates and values what each person contributes. (pp. 7–9)

Garmston (2007) distinguishes between the expert facilitator (managing process and outcome without bringing content into the conversation by staying neutral) and the citizen facilitator (managing process and outcome and bringing one's own voice into the conversation). Most grade-level or content-area teams require citizen facilitators because everyone is involved in teaching and the focus of the team. The three top responsibilities for a citizen facilitator are (1) to be a link between the principal and team, helping to communicate priorities, ideas, and recommendations; (2) to help the team grow and learn about effective team skills and behaviors; and (3) to keep the big picture and vision and facilitate the flow and outcomes of the meeting. (For more information, see Killion, 2013.) You may also see "Facilitative Leadership Competencies" at **go.solution-tree.com/plcbooks**.

Team Leader

The team leader can be the facilitator or enlist help facilitating. Some teams combine the facilitation and team leader roles with one person. The team leader's responsibilities include:

- Developing the agenda with the team
- Establishing purpose and beginning the meeting
- Referring to the product or results intended
- Recommending procedures for accomplishing the task
- Engaging every member and participating in conversation when necessary
- Protecting the norms and the agreements
- Helping name roles before and during the process
- Summarizing at different times and at the end of the meeting, and asking, "Who is doing what by when?"

The facilitator makes sure to include a meeting evaluation and closes the meeting. An effective team leader models effective communication and data use and has an action orientation.

The team leader also assumes positive intention and does not belittle other team members. When necessary, the team leader confronts and approaches difficult conversations. Good team leaders are comfortable with ambiguity and enjoy seeing the work unfold with the team. They believe in the notion that more can be achieved collectively. They have the respect and trust of their teammates and value what each member brings to the team. They can ask for help facilitating when they have very specific ideas about a topic and want to weigh in or advocate for a direction.

Recorder

The recorder captures the big ideas and topics of the team and posts them to a shared website. The recorder uses charts or a shared document to help keep the work visual and is careful to write exactly what individuals contribute. Clarifying and remaining neutral will assist individuals in feeling heard and valued. We have seen teammates become upset when their idea is not reflected. We have also seen less productivity from a team when a recorder does not keep up or take the job seriously. Effective teams create products, so the recording job is critical and can be shared throughout the meeting.

The recorder works with the summarizer throughout and at the end of the meeting to make sure important concepts and action steps are reflected. Some teams take photos of the charts to complete a record of the meeting.

Timekeeper

The timekeeper is aware of the time used for specific agenda items and reminds the team when time is almost up. Methods to alert the team include a hand raised to signal five minutes left or a verbal statement such as "five more minutes."

Process Observer

An effective team is always looking for areas in which to improve, and a process observer provides feedback to individuals or the team about operations and interactions. The process observer provides strengths and areas to improve on and points out individual contributions. He or she may also lead the team in a debrief at the end of the meeting or at a crucial time, asking participants to reflect and talk about their own actions and what they did to enhance or take away from the effectiveness of the team.

Summarizer

Helping the team transition from one topic to the next is the key role of the summarizer. After each major topic or decision, the summarizer states the key points and asks the team if they would add or change anything. It keeps everyone focused.

The summarizer works closely with the recorder to accurately reflect the team's work by writing the key statements down.

Most Responsible Person

To balance the workload, team members step up and volunteer to take on tasks. Once they volunteer, their name is recorded next to the item. They consequently become the most responsible person for that task.

Team Member

It is good to review the roles and responsibilities of team members. Sometimes, we see individuals taking a back seat, expecting others to complete the tasks. By describing what we expect, we see more of it. Reviewing the norms helps to identify several responsibilities of team members, such as actively participating in conversations and learning, catching up with another member if a meeting is missed, asking for clarification when confused, and keeping student learning at the heart of conversations. See "Continuous Improvement" at **go.solution-tree.com/plcbooks**.

Principal

The principal ensures that there is a level of reciprocity and support to the team. The principal (or designee—sometimes this is an assistant principal) will articulate, promote, and protect the mission and vision of the school. He or she is able to clarify and describe the changes being discussed and may assist teams in setting specific tasks and outcomes. He or she describes what is negotiable and non-negotiable related to the work of the team and establishes timelines and structures to support the work. The principal does not micromanage and attend all team meetings, but he or she does monitor, celebrate, and encourage a culture focused on learning. See "Slip Sliding Away" at **go.solution-tree.com/plcbooks**.

Chapter 4
Skills and Behaviors

Effective teams know the importance of learning and refining skills to support collaborative work, and they commit to continually learning and developing these skills and behaviors.

When teacher leaders are asked during professional learning or in school visits "What stops your team from working well together?" many describe experiences related to communication, interpersonal dynamics, and conflict. They also refer to negative data conversations and facilitator issues. Stories are told about the times work halted because of personality conflicts, harsh words exchanged between teammates, or someone being ignored or discounted during a meeting. Others lament about the inability to process data objectively or team members and leaders avoiding conflict and steering clear of difficult conversations. We think the stories are disheartening and unnecessary.

High-performing teams have a continuous growth orientation and ask reflective questions. They know what individual and collective strengths and weaknesses exist when collaborating. Sometimes, we receive feedback from others if we pay attention and are receptive. Other times, we observe the dynamics in our team and realize our contributions or shortcomings. A skilled administrator may provide specific accommodations and areas of growth in the formal evaluation process. All of us can grow from feedback related to how we work with others.

In a collaborative culture, it is imperative to talk about the results of our work and how we work. Skills needed to work collaboratively can be learned and practiced with each team session. Researchers and leaders in leadership and education have contributed to what works, and many skills and behaviors can be categorized under interpersonal, conflict and consensus, data, and facilitation skills.

Interpersonal Skills

Dennis Sparks (2005) writes about leadership and transformation through interpersonal influence in his book *Leading for Results*: "Individuals can have a profound influence on one another and their organization through particular kinds of interactions and creative processes" (p. xiii). We observe that high-performing teams, in addition to having goals and being focused on the right work, are also skillful in communication and interpersonal effectiveness.

Anthony Bryk and Barbara Schneider (2002), in their study of the Chicago elementary school system between 1991 and 1997, found that schools improving in student achievement had higher relational trust between adults in the building and with parents. They also found that successful schools had many of the elements of professional learning communities with a focus on student learning, adults committed to innovation and always getting better, and collaborative teams working together. The research is compelling and is highlighted in their book *Trust in Schools: A Core Resource for Improvement*. What we know is that trust is a temporary state and can change depending on the relationships and actions of those we work with. Trust is fostered and cultivated in our interactions and actions.

Listening and Speaking

Collaboration requires everyone in the team working interdependently, listening to one another with a commitment to understand. When teams collaborate on a product such as a common formative assessment and performance levels, each person will have an opinion about rigor, key concepts, and more. To ensure quality work, teammates need to listen to the commonalities and differences. Good decisions are made after exploring and learning together. We have observed teams changing their thinking and stance after listening to one another in different ways. We have also witnessed recalcitrant team members letting go of their preferred solution once they knew their teammates understood their point of view and respected it.

> Listening is a commitment and a compliment. It's a commitment to understanding how other people feel, how they see their world. It means putting aside your own prejudices and beliefs, your anxieties and self-interest, so that you can step behind the other person's eyes. You try to look at things from his or her perspective. Listening is a compliment because it says to the other person: "I care about what's happening to you; your life and your experiences are important." (McKay, Davis, & Fanning, 1983, p. 6)

Listening and participating requires a commitment to the following:

- Using wait time
- Monitoring your inner voice

- Monitoring your speaking
- Paraphrasing in authentic ways
- Clarifying
- Elaborating
- Summarizing

Using Wait Time

The research on "wait time" (silence) points out that more higher-order and complex thinking occurs when teachers provide more time for students to think about answers. The same is true for adults. When we allow pauses in conversation, more thinking will occur and more members will participate.

Monitoring Your Inner Voice

Quiet your mind and thoughts. Let go when your inner voice jumps ahead of the speaker and connects or identifies to your own personal experiences, comparing and judging a remark to your own or another's comments, filtering and listening to only parts of the conversation, and rehearsing what you may say as soon as you have an opportunity. Stay present and attend to the speaker.

Monitoring Your Speaking

"Inner talk" may lead to voicing what you are thinking. At this point, the focus shifts to you and away from the person speaking.

> *Personal Referencing* occurs when our minds shift from listening to understand another, to considering what is being said with reference to our own experiences and then judging its worth; *Personal Curiosity* when we are interested in what the protégé is saying not to understand his or her needs, but because we want more information for ourselves; *Personal Certainty* when we are sure we know the solution to the problem. (Lipton & Wellman, 2003, p. 37)

When we engage in personal referencing, curiosity, or certainty, we can become distracted from listening and begin to tell our own stories, ask more questions for ourselves, and give advice. It may distract from what the person is saying and divert the conversation. Other behaviors that may derail a conversation are statements reflecting the need to be right, changing the subject, or placating and constantly agreeing with what is being said. We have also noticed that some personalities are accustomed to challenging one another and asking questions to make a point instead of clarifying. If teamwork is not going well, we ask ourselves, Are we focused? Do we have the right structure and processes in place? Or is it more basic? Are we listening to one another in an effective manner? "One of the greatest gifts you can give another human being is to care enough to listen to their story" (Richard Leider, as quoted in Sparks, 2005, p. 72). This quote is repeated in many settings and dates back to our childhood when we are learning the basics of treating others like we want to be treated.

Paraphrasing in Authentic Ways

Let teammates know your desire to understand their point of view and their feelings. If done well and with the right intention, paraphrasing will help teammates feel listened to and more responsive for in-depth and challenging conversations. It also helps us remember what was said, moves the conversation along, and alleviates miscommunication or assumptions. Paraphrasing is stating in your own words what you think was said. Sometimes, we do it to *acknowledge*, and we can use sentence starters such as "You are feeling . . ." and "You are suggesting . . ." Other times, we are trying to *clarify* and might use starters such as "In other words . . .," "The point you are making is . . .," "So . . .," and "Do I have it correct when I say . . .?" You can check for understanding and move the meeting along when you paraphrase to *summarize*: "I hear two points. The first is . . ., the second is . . .," "So far, I have heard the following . . ." I have also observed team leaders and members paraphrase to help *organize* the thinking: "It sounds like you would suggest . . . and then . . . and then . . ." The key to paraphrasing is to not do it all the time and avoid using the statement, "So, what I hear you say is . . ." Paraphrasing can actually turn off participation if people think it is artificial. Do it naturally and with the intention to understand. Paraphrasing is not an easy skill, but it is certainly one of the most powerful.

Clarifying

Clarifying is used to increase meaning and understanding by asking questions or using sentence starters. It is important that questions are those that help us understand. Sometimes, people will say, "I have a clarifying question," and then state their idea in such a manner that they are really making a point. Their interest is to make sure people hear their point of view. When this happens, call it. Say, "I am not sure if that is a clarifying question or a point of view." If said without judgment and to be more matter of fact, team members appreciate this distinction, and it helps the conversation continue. In "Seven Norms of Collaboration" in *The Adaptive School* (Garmston & Wellman, 2009), the authors suggest using the skill and behavior "probing for specificity," which will increase clarity and more precise thinking. Phrases such as "Tell me more; I would like to hear more about . . ." and "Please say more about . . ." are good starters.

Staying open to what others say is not an easy skill, especially when we have strong opinions and beliefs about something. If we hear something that causes us to question ourselves and our thinking, we become anxious, irritated, or threatened. Our self-esteem may be endangered. The key to staying open is to hear the whole statement or story without jumping to conclusions and judging with partial information. Listening and speaking in a committed way does not mean we agree with everything said. Disagreements about facts or differing points of view need to be expressed. Our teammates will be more inclined to learn, listen, and receive feedback from us once they have the experience of being listened to.

Elaborating

Probing is another skill that surfaces more information and detail from the speaker. When more information is needed to understand, and we would like the speaker to provide more specifics and detail, we use open-ended probes: "I am interested in . . ." or "Please say more about . . ." or "I would like to hear more about . . ." (Garmston & Wellman, 2009).

Summarizing

Show understanding, move a conversation along, and provide those not in the room with a condensed version by summarizing key points. Summarizing should be used throughout the conversation to let others know you hear key points and are getting the essence of their point of view. It also helps those who may have lost their focus and didn't hear what was said. The skill also moves the group to a conclusion and helps with closure related to a topic or agenda item. Collaborative teams often summarize at the end of a session and ask the recorder or minute taker to note the key points and agreements made. Summarizing takes focus and energy and requires commitment and effort.

Challenging Conversations

The skills used to increase listening and understanding (such as deep listening, pausing, paraphrasing, probing, clarifying, elaborating, and summarizing) are the same skills used in challenging conversations. One of the Commitments of Highly Functioning Teams at Legacy High School is "We engage in unfiltered, constructive dialogue" (Legacy High School, 2015). This implies that staff and team members are forthright in their conversation. They are candid, and they express their point of view. Some call it "telling our truth." They are also willing to uncover assumptions and risk being vulnerable. They may feel nervous or intimidated at times, yet they know this commitment is key in participating in a meaningful conversation.

We recommend a structure and process when you know you are embarking on a challenging or crucial conversation. In the book *Crucial Conversations*, Kerry Patterson and colleagues (2002) write that "crucial conversations are those when opinions vary, stakes are high, and emotions run strong" (pp. 1–2). By using the process recommended by the authors (preparing well, finding mutual purpose, creating a safe environment, using dialogue as a way to create shared understanding and meaning, and brainstorming solutions), relationships improve and the parties can move beyond the issue(s).

Another source for learning how to structure and facilitate a challenging conversation is the book titled *Having Hard Conversations* by Jennifer Abrams (2009). Abrams writes about eighteen reasons we hesitate to have the hard conversation such as a desire to please, personal safety, fear of the unknown, and fatigue. She also provides tips on setting expectations, being explicit in our language, and making a plan to meet and talk. As teams collaborate and change, they will experience conflict. It is a natural by-product and outcome of those working together. Creating shared meaning and working through issues involve challenging assumptions, expressing our truth and point of view, and balancing inquiry and advocacy.

Challenging Assumptions

Assumptions are ideas we hold true but may not be. Our stories, experiences, and imaginations combine to create our assumptions, and they may guide us in our actions. When we are working collaboratively, we place ideas on the table and state our truth. In the process of exploring, we may make assumptions or we may hear an assumption that needs to be challenged. Use a gentle probe or provide a statement such as "I wonder if what we are talking about is more of an assumption. Can you describe how you came to think about it this way?" It is not necessary to yell, "You just don't get it!" or "You are wrong!" Assumptions about what is the best approach to teaching and learning occur often and are held very personally by educators. Approached the wrong way, teachers will tend to dig in their heels rather than open their minds to new ideas. Often, team agreements to try something new will force someone to try a strategy or approach he or she would never have done on his or her own. Team members must model the open mind they expect from their colleagues. Trying an idea provided by the intractable person on your team and giving him or her feedback on what you liked about it can serve to build trust. Data also provide an objective reference point for either confirming or denying one's assumptions.

Expressing Your Truth and Point of View

Don't hold back. If you want to create more open conversation and trust, say what is on your mind. Expressing your point of view requires courage to speak your mind and to describe the situation or idea from your perspective. Chadwick (2012) reminds us that what we see and experience is "our truth." He illustrates this in his workshops and sessions by placing four chairs facing different directions in a room and asking what each person would see if asked to describe the room from their perspective. One might see the windows and describe the view of trees, blue sky, and nature. Another might see a door, an exit sign, and food. Another may see a group of apprehensive and unsmiling people, and the last may see a group of animated and active people having a conversation. Do they all observe facts? Are the descriptions different? Are they "truth" to the person describing the room?

What if we only heard one or two of the descriptions? We would not have a very accurate picture of the room. The example illustrates that teams need all parts and pieces to a story to understand the whole, and it also illustrates that sometimes we do not have all the information. We only know what we have observed or learned. We need to widen our vision and learn more. When we express our point of view or tell our truth, we may show others that we lack complete or accurate information. We may not have all the answers. It is OK. Breathe deep. Go for it. If you describe your view respectfully, without condemnation for others' views, and seek input after you have spoken, teammates will respond with admiration. Use starters such as "I am seeing it differently. I would like to provide my perspective, and when I am finished, I would like to hear what others think"; "I have come to an understanding about this, and I would like to provide my perspective"; "I have heard many ideas expressed, and I am learning a lot. I would like to state what I am thinking too." Effective teams are appreciative of those who dare to take a risk, providing their point of view and at the same time modeling vulnerability and transparency.

Balancing Inquiry and Advocacy

Dialogue can be described as listening to learn. Teams that use dialogue to explore an idea foster participation and see positive results including shifts in mental models and mindsets. Dialogue requires the skill of inquiry.

Asking questions, investigating, and learning are at the heart of inquiry. When teams use inquiry and explore a topic in depth without coming to conclusions prematurely, they build shared understanding and consensus for a solution. Inquiry means staying open and suspending judgment, listening to learn, and not advocating for a personal choice. It does not mean arguing and debating. It requires discipline and process to ensure all voices are heard and members have said what they need to say. Inquiry is best used in the early stages of a new idea and precedes making decisions.

Recommending and speaking in favor of an idea describes advocacy. If done poorly, teammates may be turned off to the speaker. When done well, the person championing the idea and advocating may convince others to agree with all or part of the message. Advocating requires gathering facts, arranging thoughts in a concrete and logical fashion, and speaking with clarity. Telling stories and providing examples may appeal to emotions and heart. Some use advocacy as they build a case for change. The focusing four strategy by Garmston and Wellman (2009) assists teams in getting to a decision using advocacy as a primary step. A common mistake associated with advocacy is using it too frequently and too early in the process of a conversation or a decision-making process. When a person tries to sell his or her idea without listening to options and respecting others' points of view, team members may not be willing to be convinced. We have observed anger and blocking when advocating becomes the norm of communication in teams. Advocate at the right time, with succinct information, and with clarity. Know your teammates and how they receive your words. Keep your voice strong and confident without using authoritative and argumentative tones. Also, understand the meanings of *debate* and *argue* in the context of a team.

Synonyms for *debate* are *discuss, argue, hash out,* and *dispute*. The concept of debate evokes memories of courtrooms, city council meetings, or elections. Debate is most often a formal discussion on a particular topic in a public meeting. However, as used in the context of team meetings, it refers to contentious issues. For some teams, debate becomes a communication pattern and arguing becomes a norm. Arguing can be associated with the practice in courtrooms with each side providing evidence and persuading others. Most often, it is associated with escalated voices, quarrels, and feuding. We all have different experiences with arguments from our childhood through our adult lives. Arguments may cause a fight-or-flight response, depending on one's personal history with arguing. Team members may choose flight and withdraw their participation, avoid or not show up to meetings, or leave meetings early. Others may choose fight and use their debate skills to belittle another point of view and to win at all costs. The rate, tone, and inflections in voice may change, and voices may get faster, louder, and even sarcastic. Relationships can get damaged. What replaces debating and arguing? Recommit to effective communication skills and change the dynamics. Use intentional processes, protocols, roles, and skills.

Consensus and Conflict Skills

Again, we go back to basics and use the power of effective communication skills when there is a conflict and varying perspectives about an idea. We also use focus and structure to ensure an effective approach. In addition, we build knowledge and reflect on our relationship to conflict. Do we see conflict as a resource to facilitate increased understanding and divergent points of view? Do we view it as an opportunity to surface perceptions and misunderstandings? Do we know it is a necessary outcome of people working collaboratively? Or do we blame others, run, hide, or cringe when faced with conflict? Increasing our cognitive skills about conflict is helpful. It increases our resourcefulness in order to contribute positively to our team. Let's look at an example.

Conflict began to occur between Sarah and members of the Mountain Middle School math team. A comment was made during one of the meetings by Rita, a teammate: "Sarah, you do not seem to care about the team norms and commitments." Roberto followed in an exasperated voice and cited three different times Sarah had not fulfilled her responsibilities to the team: "You didn't attend last month, you were late last Wednesday, and you did not give the common assessment the same time the rest of the team did." Sarah was put on the spot, became defensive, and lashed out at him. She turned red and was close to being in tears. It was clear she was also upset. Instead of working through the issue, the team changed the subject, hurried through the rest of the agenda, and left the meeting early.

Upon leaving, team members began to talk about the incident in the parking lot, and predictably, many staff members soon became aware that there was conflict on the math team. Sarah immediately went to her science colleagues and vented about her frustrations. Teachers started approaching other teachers and defending Sarah and criticizing Rita and Roberto for being so rude in the meeting. People were taking sides and criticizing, and the conflict escalated. Within a week, Sarah asked to leave the math team. She felt singled out by the team and unsupported.

Types of Conflict

When teams disagree or voice differing points of view about a substantive issue, idea, value, or commitment, it is called *cognitive conflict*. It is considered healthy and normal and can lead to new understandings and better decisions. Of course, talking through differences requires process and honed communication skills, and many teams struggle in this area. A more destructive type of conflict is *affective conflict*. Comments become personal and hurtful. Statements are made that attack or question another person. Negative comments can lead to distrust and alienation.

Adriana, the team leader, knew she needed to facilitate the team having a conversation about what happened and how they could move beyond it. She also knew it would require work to bring Rita, Roberto, and Sarah together again and decrease all the friction and noise within the team and throughout the staff. One of the first steps she took was to seek Sarah out and let her know that the team valued her and wanted her to stay engaged and contributing. Leaving the team was not an option, so their mutual interest was working together effectively and collaboratively. Adriana used her communication skills and empathized and listened to Sarah. She paraphrased to let Sarah know she understood her feelings and heard her insights and words. She also asked why Sarah had struggled with some of the norms. After some time, she suggested a conversation with Rita, Roberto, and the team so they could move beyond the situation. Sarah was reluctant at first, but after talking to her principal and thinking about the importance of working things out, she knew she needed to participate in such a meeting.

Sources of Conflict

Misunderstanding, miscommunication, scarcity, power, ego, values, and change can all be sources of conflict. Strong emotions can interfere with the ability to uncover the sources behind the conflict. It often takes a facilitated conversation and telling the story from different perspectives to understand what happened. One way to do this is to bring the team together to listen to each other's perspective, to acknowledge the hurt and pain caused, to explore interests and options, and to move to a new place. Often the interest-based strategies method described in chapter 2 can be used or modified. The consensus model by Chadwick (2012) will lead a team step by step through a conversation or a series of conversations.

Adriana set the stage for the conversation and described mutual purpose, expectations for the meeting, and important norms to keep in mind. She asked the team to check in with their hopes and expectations for the conversation and asked three members including Sarah to begin by describing the situation and how they felt about it. Sarah stated, "I felt attacked and misunderstood. I have heard that people are calling me uncommitted and a slacker. I am a member of both the science and math teams, and it isn't working in my schedule. Both teams meet at the same time. I feel like I am always behind the rest of the team, and I can't do my job well. It isn't fair to me or to the kids." She acknowledged she should have worked out her dilemma of being on two teams before she started to miss meetings and team commitments.

Rita provided her perspective and stated, "There probably was a better way to address what I thought were violations of our norms. I didn't even ask you why." Roberto apologized for his accusing tone in the conversation and yet was still concerned. "We have said that as a team, it is OK to confront behaviors that violate the norms. I thought I was upholding the values of the team by saying something." As others brought their perspectives in and described both the incident and what occurred in the parking lot and throughout the school, new insights and observations were made that led to understanding. They identified the sources of the conflict including poor choices in communication, lack of time to do everything that needed to be done, lack of communication early on, misunderstandings, and lack of personal regard. The issue took on a life of its own, and the team acknowledged that they need better processes and more attention to their own personal communication.

Preferences and Responses to Conflict

People have different responses once conflict occurs. In addition to fight or flight, some avoid, others tried to direct or control, and yet others begin to harmonize and seek cooperation. The importance of the task and relationship provokes different responses.

After the math team explored the situation telling their stories without interruption and judgments by others and offering insights, Adriana asked them to describe their worst fear if they didn't move beyond the conflict and their best hope if they did. (See "Best Hopes and Worst Fears" on page 20.) Once they processed this activity, they moved on and talked about behaviors and strategies to foster their best hopes. Suggestions were made such as: create a learning partner system to help absent members stay involved and informed when they do miss, talk to the science team about alternative schedules, support one another by asking better questions, avoid assumptions, presume positive intention, don't accuse, use "I statements" when describing instead of "you statements," do the work in the room and not in the parking lot, and don't talk to others before talking to the person directly involved.

To end the meeting, she asked the team members to voice their commitment and to describe what they would each personally do to help the team move forward. The team also agreed (with Sarah's support) that they would share a brief comment with other teachers not on the team, that they now understood some of the factors and conditions that had led to the issue, and that the math team was back on track. The meeting was adjourned after the go around and hearing from each person how he or she would help the team work together in the future.

Paralanguage and Meta Messages

Paralanguage is "the vocal component of speech, considered apart from the verbal content. It includes pitch, resonance, articulation, tempo, volume and rhythm" (McKay et al., 1983, p. 69).

Unintentionally, we communicate our frustrations as well as our preferences through our sounds. Our attitude is revealed and may have a positive or negative impact on the team. When teams are struggling with difficult issues or stressed for time, a tone may set a person off in a negative way. Recently, we watched a member of a team ask a question, and the tone was interpreted as dissatisfaction. Members reacted and became combative and defensive. As the conflict started to emerge, the person initiating quickly pointed out that the question was not meant to criticize and apologized because that wasn't the intent. It was healthy that awareness of the behavior occurred and the person took responsibility. However, the key is to stay more conscious with our paralanguage choices and avoid a possible reaction.

Voice

Use your voice in your team to make a statement or to elicit more conversation.

Tone, inflections, rate, and volume do matter. Use the credible voice to make a point and call for attention. Use the approachable voice to pique interest and involvement. Michael Grinder describes that our voice patterns will fall somewhere on a continuum between cred-

> ibility on one end and approachability on the other. The credible voice pattern is used to send information and increase importance. It is characterized by more pauses, intonations that curl down at the end of a statement or word, and the speaker's head holding still when delivering the message. The approachable voice includes more head nodding, more rhythmic patterns, and intonations that curl up on the end of a statement or word. (Sparks, 2008, p. 52)

Pay attention to how you talk and how the message is delivered. Pay more attention to the reactions by teammates. Do they shut down, react defensively, or continue to participate?

Body Language

Paying attention to our body language is essential because over 50 percent of the message's impact comes from body language and movements. Albert Mehrabian has found that the total impact of a message breaks down like this: 7 percent is verbal (words), 38 percent is vocal (volume, pitch, rhythm, and such), and 55 percent is body movements (mostly facial expressions) (McKay et al., 1983). Grinder (1997) reminds us that most of what is communicated is apart from words.

To help the team feel more relaxed during stressful times, gesture with your palms up to invite participation. When someone does raise his or her voice or begins to repeat his or her message, bring your hands above the table with palms down and keep them still for a moment. At the same time, use that credible and gentle voice and paraphrase or name what is happening. In addition, breathe deep. Others will pick up on it consciously or unconsciously and begin to relax.

Data Conversation Skills

In addition to the roles and responsibilities described in chapter 3, the skillful facilitator is attentive to adult learners and knows when to push, when to pull, and when to let go. A facilitator's job is to help the team accomplish its work and keep the team focused on student learning. In addition to modeling the communication and consensus skills, the facilitator uses data as a primary tool for creating a results orientation. The facilitator helps create a culture of learning and not a culture of intimidation and fear. Jason Cianfrance, math team leader at Legacy High School, articulates the actions and skills an effective facilitator will use in data conversations:

> The facilitator must be the guiding force that prevents data discussions from falling into the easy traps of excuse making, false modesty and hurt feelings. Facilitators must always frame data discussions with a reminder of the purpose—to improve student learning/achievement. Consistently remind teachers that data discussions, which involve comparing teacher performance, are NOT

for comparing teachers. They are for generating collegial discussions on sharing practices and strategies, which will hopefully benefit students.

Teams must have clear and understandable data to use, and they must have at least a basic statistical grounding. This is huge. Many times teams make statistically inaccurate statements, or come to inappropriate conclusions about data, and then make important decisions based on these flawed analyses. Team members must have some statistical sophistication beyond the ability to calculate an average, and many teachers are cautious and wary to jump into conversations involving statistics. Inaccurate statements abound, such as, "Wow, your class average was 81% and mine was 79%. What did you do to perform better than me?" (Likely, there is no statistical difference in these scores.) "We have a goal to increase student performance on the assessment by 3 standard deviations." (Not a reasonable or achievable goal—statistically highly unlikely.) I have heard many observations from teachers and principals that reflected misunderstandings and misconceptions. This does not mean that a college level sophistication with data is needed. As an example, consider two classes that have the same average of 75% on an assessment. Without further drilling down, these two can easily be seen as equal in performance. A deeper look into the numbers might reveal that the standard deviations, ranges, or medians of these classes differ significantly. The implications of these factors are important and not hard to understand. Teachers at all levels and with all backgrounds can handle the thinking involved in accurate analysis for the kinds of data with which they will be dealing. They just need training, time and practice.

There is hope. I have seen it addressed by schools by creating release time for facilitators and team leaders to work together and/ or with a data coach with a background in statistics. This can be very helpful in the beginning with using data and will build more accuracy and confidence in a team. In addition, it is best to use, display, and disaggregate the data different ways. Always displaying the straight percentage bar graphs for each teacher, or always using data as a way to evaluate the test questions, gets stale and boring (besides not having much deep meaning). Some ideas for alternate data discussions or formats include:

- Linking assessment questions to standards or essential concepts and then comparing whole-team data on the results of each concept.

- Comparing performance year-to-year on similar assessments.

- Grouping results by students (all of the students who got each letter grade, for example) instead of by teacher. This data can then be used for differentiation purposes or for forming heterogeneous collaborative teams for upcoming lessons.

- Thinking forward instead of backward with data. Pick a few questions that are fundamentals for success in future units and use them as a signpost for whether you are headed in the right direction. Modify upcoming instruction accordingly.

- Have conversations about how to share data results with students appropriately and in a meaningful way. Can they each be given their individual results broken down by standard? Can they see their results as compared to a team average? How can students use these results to improve their understanding?

- Ranking students on multiple parameters, such as skill level vs. conceptual understanding, in order to analyze what sorts of instruction should come next.

Keeping a creative and open mind is vital. Different subjects and topics and assessment structures will lend themselves to different kinds of data discussions. Don't be afraid to experiment and try new things. Effective teams use data as a check up and not an autopsy. I learned from a colleague, Zach Jones, that the data conversation can be "flipped." At the beginning of a current year's unit, teams can have a data discussion using last year's data on the same unit. This is a much more powerful use of data than just waiting until this year's test is over and then conducting the autopsy. Also, if data can be collected quickly and efficiently, then discussions on formative assessments can be used to make mid-course corrections during the learning process, before the summative assessment. Clear decisions and goals should result from data discussions. Having technology resources at the school such as *Mastery Manager* or *Global PD* from Solution Tree helps immensely. Having a basic comfort level with the technology, along with a willingness to explore the features available, will allow the facilitator to use the resources to their capacity. In other words, if all you are doing is using the technology to quickly scan and grade the tests, you are not using all the resources at hand. Again, practicing using the technology with other facilitators breeds more skill and confidence.

Open-Ended Questions and Specific Language

Becoming more succinct and accurate in our data conversations takes practice and skill.

Stating our observations in descriptive, nonjudgmental terms may seem like a relatively easy thing to do, but it can be one of the most challenging skills. . . . Most of us have deeply ingrained habits of perception and speech that lead us to infer, assume, and speculate rather than simply note what our senses reveal to us. (Sparks, 2005, p. 80)

Provide facts, data, and your own interpretation. Do it in a thoughtful manner without a tone that says "my truth is the truth." Note the difference between what seems to be facts and your opinions. "Meditational questions that invite and open thinking build collaborative capacities, expand the possibilities and promote ownership of ideas and actions" (Lipton & Wellman, 2004, p. 31). In their book *Data-Driven Dialogue*, Lipton and Wellman (2004) suggest that learning-focused facilitators create questions before the meeting and for different purposes. For activating and engaging thinking, use verbs such as *recall, estimate, speculate, predict,* and *wonder*. For exploring and discovering, use *observe, describe, analyze, compare,* and *contrast*, and for organizing and integrating use *evaluate, classify*, and *summarize*. Keep teammates from drawing conclusions too quickly and using language that is harsh or shuts down the dialogue. Invitational stems that can be used include: "What are some . . .," "What seems . . .," "What are your hunches about . . .," "What are some possible . . .," "How might these . . .," and "What is your sense of . . ." (Lipton & Wellman, 2004, p. 32).

Stay away from vague language and generalizations. If someone says, "The students are not using the basic elements of writing," pull the sentence apart to understand: Which students? What basic elements and at what proficiency? When and where in their writing? Do this in a way that elaborates and clarifies. We achieve a focus on learning and results when we speak with detail and specifics.

Chapter 5
Conclusion

Michael Fullan and Andy Hargreaves (1991) remind us, "Improving schools requires the creation of collaborative cultures. Without the collaborative skills and relationships, it is not possible to learn and to continue to learn as much as you need to know to improve."

Collaboration is essential to improvement in professional practice.

> When teachers work together, they improve their practice in two important ways. First, they sharpen their pedagogy by sharing specific instructional strategies for teaching more effectively. Second, they deepen their content knowledge by identifying the specific standards students must master. In other words, when teachers work together, they become better teachers. (Many & Sparks-Many, 2015, p. 83)

They explore new ways of approaching teaching and learning. Studies have also found that working on collaborative teams generated positive changes in teacher attitudes. Gallimore, Ermeling, Saunders, and Goldenberg (2009) noted that teachers working on collaborative teams were more likely to attribute gains in student achievement to improved instructional practice rather than to external factors such as student traits or socioeconomic status. In contrast, teachers who did not work on collaborative teams had the opposite experience and tended to attribute achievement gains to factors outside of their control.

> I used to be in a school that didn't believe in or foster collaboration. When we had a team meeting, my colleagues couldn't wait to leave. We never talked about the important things. It was the hardest and loneliest year of my life and I thought about leaving the profession. Instead, I applied at a school known for its excellent results with students and being a professional learning community. I am so fortunate I had a choice and could change schools. It was the best decision of my professional career and I have become a better teacher because of it. Now when I go to

a team meeting, we do meaningful work. We are clear on what students should know and be able to do, we create common assessments and we uncover what works and doesn't work for kids. We know our students are more successful and the data prove it. I will never go back to a school where I work behind closed doors and by myself. (Jason Cianfrance, personal communication, 2015)

References

Abrams, J. (2009). *Having hard conversations*. Thousand Oaks, CA: Corwin Press.

Aronson, E., & Patnoe, S. (2011). *Cooperation in the classroom: The jigsaw method* (2nd ed.). London: Pinter & Martin.

Bryk, A., & Schneider, B. (2002). *Trust in schools: A core resource for improvement*. New York: Russell Sage Foundation.

Chadwick, R. (2012). *Finding new ground: Beyond conflict to consensus*. Terrebonne, OR: One Tree.

Conzemius, A. E., & O'Neill, J. (2014). *The handbook for SMART school teams: Revitalizing best practices for collaboration* (2nd ed.). Bloomington, IN: Solution Tree Press.

Costa, A., & Garmston, R. (1994). *Cognitive coaching: A foundation for renaissance schools*. Norwood, MA: Christopher-Gordon.

Delehant, A. M. (2007). *Making meetings work: How to get started, get going, and get it done*. Thousand Oaks, CA: Corwin Press.

DuFour, R., DuFour, R., Eaker, R., & Many, T. (2010). *Learning by doing: A handbook for professional learning communities at work* (2nd ed.). Bloomington, IN: Solution Tree Press.

Easton, L. B. (2009). *Protocols for professional learning*. Alexandria, VA: Association for Supervision and Curriculum Development.

Eikenberry, K. (2012, October 24). The most misused tool in meetings [Web log post]. Accessed at http://blog.kevineikenberry.com/leadership-supervisory-skills /the-most-misused-tool-in-meetings on March 14, 2015.

Fullan, M., & St. Germain, C. (2006). *Learning places: A field guide for improving the context of schooling*. Thousand Oaks, CA: Corwin Press.

Fullan, M., & Hargreaves, A. (1991). *What's worth fighting for?: Working together for your school*. Toronto, Ontario, Canada: Public School Teachers Federation.

Gallimore, R., Ermeling, B. A., Saunders, W. M., & Goldenberg, C. (2009). Moving the learning of teaching closer to practice: Teacher education implications of school-based inquiry teams. *Elementary School Journal, 109*(3), 537–553.

Garmston, R. (2007, Summer). The citizen facilitator can keep a small group moving toward a goal. *Journal of Staff Development*, 57–58.

Garmston, R., & Wellman, B. (2009). *The adaptive school: A sourcebook for developing collaborative groups* (2nd ed.). Norwood, MA: Christopher-Gordon.

Goleman, D. (2006). *Emotional intelligence: Why it can matter more than IQ* (10th anniversary ed.). New York: Bantam Books.

Gregory, G. H., & Kuzmich, L. (2007). *Teacher teams that get results: 61 strategies for sustaining and renewing professional learning communities.* Thousand Oaks, CA: Corwin Press.

Grinder, M. (1997). *The elusive obvious: The science of non-verbal communication.* Battle Ground, WA: M. Grinder & Associates.

Kaner, S., Lind, L., Fisk, S., & Berger, D. (2007). *Facilitator's guide to participatory decision-making.* San Francisco: Jossey-Bass.

Kanold, T. D. (2011). *The five disciplines of PLC leaders.* Bloomington, IN: Solution Tree Press.

Killion, J. (2013). *School-based professional learning for implementing the Common Core.* Accessed at http://learningforward.org/docs/default-source/commoncore/tplteams.pdf on March 12, 2015.

Larner, M. (2007). *Tools for leaders: Indispensable graphic organizers, protocols, and planning guidelines for working and learning together.* New York: Scholastic.

Legacy High School. (2015). *Legacy action guide* (2nd ed.). Broomfield, CO: Author.

Lipton, L., & Wellman, B. (2003). *Mentoring matters: A practical guide to learning-focused relationships* (2nd ed.). Sherman, CT: MiraVia.

Lipton, L., & Wellman, B. (2004). *Data-driven dialogue: A facilitator's guide to collaborative inquiry.* Sherman, CT: MiraVia.

Many, T., & Sparks-Many, S. (2015). *Leverage: Using PLCs to promote lasting improvement in schools.* Thousand Oaks, CA: Corwin Press.

McKay, M., Davis, M., & Fanning, P. (1983). *Messages: The communication skills book.* Oakland, CA: New Harbinger.

Moir, E. (2008). *Ask Ellen: Collaboration is at the heart of PLCs.* Accessed at www.edutopia.org/ask-ellen-professional-learning-communities on March 10, 2015.

Muhammad, A. (2013, September 10). Building team efficacy [Web log post]. Accessed at www.allthingsplc.info/blog/view/227/building-team-efficacy on March 10, 2015.

Patterson, K., Grenny, J., McMillan, R., & Switzler, A. (2002). *Crucial conversations: Tools for talking when stakes are high.* New York: McGraw-Hill.

Rutherford, P., Kaylor, B., Clayton, H., McVicker, J., Oliver, B., Stephens-Carter, S., et al. (2011). *Creating a culture for learning: Your guide to PLCs and more.* Alexandria, VA: Just ASK Publications & Professional Development.

Sagor, R. (2000). *Guiding school improvement with action research.* Alexandria, VA: Association for Supervision and Curriculum Development.

Schwartz, P. (1991). *The art of the long view*. New York: Doubleday.

Sparks, D. (2005). *Leading for results: Transforming teaching, learning, and relationships in schools*. Thousand Oaks, CA: Corwin Press.

Sparks, S. K. (2008). Creating intentional collaboration. In C. Erkens, C. Jakicic, L. G. Jessie, D. King, S. V. Kramer, T. W. Many, et al., *The collaborative teacher: Working together as a professional learning community* (pp. 31–56). Bloomington, IN: Solution Tree Press.

Thompson-Grove, G. (2004). *What? So what? Now what?* Accessed at www.nsrf harmony.org/system/files/protocols/what_so_what_0.pdf on March 14, 2015.

Tschannen-Moran, M. (2004). *Trust matters: Leadership for successful schools*. San Francisco: Jossey-Bass.

Weaver-Dunne, D. (n.d.). *Teachers learn from looking together at student work*. Accessed at www.educationworld.com/a_curr/curr246.shtml on February 16, 2015.

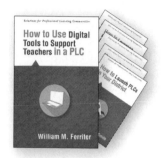

Solutions for Professional Learning Communities

The *Solutions Series* offers practitioners easy-to-implement recommendations on each book's topic—professional learning communities, digital classrooms, or modern learning. In a short, reader-friendly format, these how-to guides equip K–12 educators with the tools they need to take their school or district to the next level.

How to Use Digital Tools to Support Teachers in a PLC
William M. Ferriter
BKF675

How to Leverage PLCs for School Improvement
Sharon V. Kramer
BKF668

How to Coach Leadership in a PLC
Marc Johnson
BKF667

How to Develop PLCs for Singletons and Small Schools
Aaron Hansen
BKF676

How to Cultivate Collaboration in a PLC
Susan K. Sparks and Thomas W. Many
BKF678

How to Launch PLCs in Your District
W. Richard Smith
BKF665

Wait! Your professional development journey doesn't have to end with the last pages of this book.

We realize improving student learning doesn't happen overnight. And your school or district shouldn't be left to puzzle out all the details of this process alone.

No matter where you are on the journey, we're committed to helping you get to the next stage.

Take advantage of everything from **custom workshops** to **keynote presentations** and **interactive web and video conferencing**. We can even help you develop an action plan tailored to fit your specific needs.

Let's get the conversation started.

Call 888.763.9045 today.